Geo

MW01235041

How
Implication Binds
And
Silence Forbids

Studies in Biblical Hermeneutics

Foreword by
William Woodson

Published by

PC Publications
2545 Madrono
Ann Arbor, Michigan 48103

Library of Congress Catalog Card Number: 98-96828

ISBN 0-9669247-0-3

Printed in the United States by
Morris Publishing • 3212 East Highway 30 • Kearney, NE 68847

Dedication

This book is dedicated to
Gerald H. Beals and Rose Beals,
dad and mom,
in loving memory.

About the Author

George F. Beals was born on September 17, 1944, and grew up in Brockton, Massachusetts. He married Marion Walters from Quincy, Massachusetts. The couple has one daughter, Susan. George has an Associate degree in Electronic Engineering Technology from Northeastern University in Boston, a BA in Classics (ancient Greek and Latin) from the University of New Hampshire in Durham, New Hampshire (*summa cum laude*), and an MA in Near Eastern Studies from the University of Michigan in Ann Arbor. He also graduated from the Preston Road School of Preaching in Dallas, Texas in 1971 (Eldred Stevens, Director).

George has served churches of Christ as an evangelist and Bible school teacher in Texas, New Hampshire, Pennsylvania and Michigan.

To pay the bills, George has been a technical writer for over 20 years in the computer and automotive industries. He has served as a writing consultant in the MBA program for the University of Michigan in Ann Arbor, and is a senior member of the Society for Technical Communication.

Table of Contents

Acknowledgements

I want to thank especially the following people who helped me in the writing of this book. (Of course, any mistakes found are to be attributed to me, not to these folks.) Thomas Marshall, now evangelist in Richmond, VA, and Bob Peterson, now in Centerville, MA, for teaching me and loved ones the saving message, for which I shall be eternally grateful; the adult Bible class of the Saline, Michigan church of Christ; you reasoned together with me in class about the subject matter of this book; Marie Stolarick, a sister in Christ and friend, for your volunteering, patience and encouragement in typing and editing the manuscript, and for artwork suggestions; L.V. Pfeifer, for that wonderful course on the NT church at Preston Road, your patience with my newness there, and your recent, encouraging comments regarding this book; Thomas Warren for your work and publications over the years for the Lord's Cause, and for personal conversations, encouragement and friendship in more recent years. (In Part 1, to illustrate implication, I borrow Tom's helpful observation that none of our name's is found in the Bible); William Woodson, for reviewing the manuscript, for our conversations, for your insightful comments and challenges, your suggestions, your foreword, and your friendship; Perry B. Cotham, for your comments and your frequent mentioning of this book to others; I have become friends with Tom, William and Perry only in recent years; I wish we had met earlier in life; my wife Marion and daughter Sue, for their patience with me during the writing of this book; all other reviewers and those who listened to me with interest on these subjects, and who prodded me on toward publication!

Notes to Readers

See the items in *For Study and Discussion* beginning on page 252. These aim at helping you to understand the basic concepts progressively through the book. The items are divided into three sets: One each for Parts 1, 2 and 3. If you are using this book in a class, consider this: For the first class, overview the book using the table of contents as a guide. For each subsequent class, assign reading and the corresponding number of items from *For Study and Discussion* to be discussed in that class. Go over the reading, supplementing it with your own observations.

Bible quotations are from the *New King James Version* (Thomas Nelson, Inc., 1982)

When I provide a quotation, unless otherwise noted, I have sought to retain the original author's emphases.

The quotations I provide in the book largely are from members of the churches of Christ or others touching the Restoration Movement (Christian Church, Disciples of Christ,...). You may want to add more from other sources. And, of course, any Biblical principle established is useful to all.

Foreword

This book by George F. Beals, *How Implication Binds and Silence Forbids,* breaks new ground in some areas developed and pushes forward studies which have been brought to a certain point by earlier writers. It is, therefore, a very important book and deserves most careful study.

Implication

The oft heard statement that the Bible teaches by command, by approved example, and by implication, while well known in our heritage, has been under considerable fire by some among us in recent years - especially the binding nature of implication. George Beals thoroughly sustains the fact that implication in Scripture binds the will of God. Several contemporary denials of the binding nature of biblical implications are noted and critiqued; Bible passages which teach implicit, binding truth are discussed in some detail.

Silence

"Where the Scriptures are silent, we are silent" is well known among us, but it is explained in two sharply different ways: Silence forbids what is not taught; silence gives permission to do what is not taught. How can one be sure which explanation of this summary statement is right? Beals distinguishes between Bible "silence" and Bible "implication" very carefully, discusses numerous verses concerning this theme (2 Tim. 3:16, 17; 1 Thess. 5:21; Col. 3:17; Heb. 1:4-5; 1:13; 5:1-10; 7:13-14; 8:4-5; 13:10-11), and concludes: "So when there is silence, there is no affirmation. Therefore, Bible silence is also a subset of the Bible-unauthorized." Numerous diagrams are presented to clarify and visually emphasize the proof that Bible silence forbids. Here, especially, the book goes beyond various earlier studies and breaks the way into new, though true, insights on this valuable theme. Critique is given to the claim of many contemporary writers that Bible silence permits rather than forbids; numerous additional verses which show Bible silence forbids are discussed; "what does the forbidding" is detailed most carefully, and objections are rebutted. Closing comments and applications are provided.

The urgent importance of noting the truth that "Bible silence forbids" emerges from a teaching experience I had with a young man some time ago. This young man is a Christian, has completed several years of training in environmental engineering, is well educated, and is very quick of wit. Also, he has studied carefully various Christian Church defenses of instrumental music in worship, with, I maintain, much resultant confusion and difficulty.

In the discussion, I underscored the fact that the Bible authorizes the church to "sing" in worship (Eph. 5:19; Col. 3:16), but no teaching in Scripture authorizes instrumental music in worship. He constantly stated that, from his reading, brethren maintain that instrumental music is prohibited by the word "sing;" but this, he rightly observed, is a mistake in logical analysis. He had difficulty in putting his point in exact statements, but it was clear he could not and did not agree that "sing" prohibits "play," and there the matter was stuck.

This fine young man, however, was virtually floored by my statements that while some have argued for the prohibition or interdiction of instrumental music by NT references to "singing," this is neither the representative stance among brethren nor the best line of argument for singing and against playing instrumental music in worship. The real issue, I emphasized, is the lack of New Testament authority for instrumental music in the worship of the church; it is wrong to

xii

use instrumental music because there is no NT authority for it! It was noted that if Scripture authorized instrumental music in the worship of the church as it does "singing," there would be no contradiction between the two sets of passages; but the reality is no verses so authorize instrumental music.

It took some two hours or so to get the distinction between NT authority for "singing," no NT authority for "playing" instrumental music in worship, and the truth that the argument on "singing" does not prohibit "playing" if there were NT authority to play instrumental music in worship clearly fixed in his mind. His confusion was the result of the faulty line of argumentation that "sing" forbids "play." It was shown this is not the proper line of argumentation and is not the truth of Scripture. The point is still very important to understand and clarify.

While this incident underscores one dimension of this book which Beals has discussed most thoroughly, it is but one part of this fine book - extremely valuable though it is for this argumentation alone. I constantly thought of this fine book in manuscript as I discussed these matters with this fine young man.

Finally, this book well deserves careful consideration of faithful brethren for three important reasons, out of many which could be cited. First, George Beals is a faithful Christian husband, father and preacher. A native of Massachusetts, George has faithfully and diligently served in churches of Christ around Ann Arbor, Michigan and elsewhere for the last twenty or so years. He is effective in his ministry, trusted and appreciated by brethren in the area, and diligent in the work of the local church.

Second, this book discusses vital matters concerning the understanding and application of the Bible to the Christian life and the work of the church. Also, it guides us well in the resistance to various forms of doctrinal error, from the Christian Church use of instrumental music in worship to the false claims and encroachments of change agents among churches of Christ. One who does not clearly and fully understand these principles of Bible interpretation will be ill-prepared to discuss vital themes with capable spokesmen for these expressions of error - as well as denominational error in general. He has rendered good service in clarifying and guiding us in the use of these insights.

Third, George is well qualified and has written a well crafted discussion of these vital themes. He has studied well in colleges from Northeastern University to the University of Michigan, is a technical writer of manuals in the highly competitive computer industry, frequently researches material available in the fine library of the University of Michigan and is well acquainted with current developments and problems within our great brotherhood. He has written with these forms of expertise at his fingertips; the result is a well written, clearly illustrated, technically accurate, and well crafted statement of the case he has maintained. It is a pleasure to call him friend as well as brother.

William Woodson
Lawrenceburg, Tennessee
July 1, 1998

Part 1:
Implication

There is the view that only the Bible's explicit teachings can rightly be bound on people. That is, we are being told that we must not bind implication on one another. As one name for this view I will introduce the term the *explicit-only doctrine*. Notice at the outset the difficulty in which those who affirm this doctrine entangle themselves: When they claim this, they thereby inform us that nothing **they** are telling us, including this very claim, can rightly be bound, except any relevant word-for-word statements they might include from the Bible! Not a one can be consistent with his own claim.

One clear way of showing that the *bind-no-implication* doctrine (the "explicit-only" doctrine) is false is to show the futility in attempting to defend it. So in Part 1, I will focus on one author's book in which he expresses this doctrine.

In its entirety, Part 1 covers the following areas:

- Explain clearly what implication is (Chapter 1).
- Provide quotations from a representative author who expresses the explicit-only doctrine. It is important that I do this so you will see exactly what the author is teaching in his own words (Chapter 2).
- Prove that this view of implication is unscriptural, has serious spiritual consequences, and must be resisted. And, thus, its alternative (that the Bible teaches explicitly **and implicitly**) must be true and promoted. (Chapters 3-6).
- Gather additional quotations, and in some cases provide a critique of these as well (Chapters 7-9). Admittedly, to prove the point, it is not necessary to go through the words of others who teach the same doctrine. But I thought you would find it helpful to browse other expressions of it, as well as to see "where it's coming from."

Chapter 1
What Implication Is

Statement A implies statement B when it is impossible for statement A to be true *and* for statement B to be false. In other words, one statement (or a combination of statements) implies a second statement when the truthfulness of the first guarantees the truthfulness of the second.[1] Statement A (or the combination of statements) is called "evidence," statement B is called the "conclusion," and both together are called a logical "argument."[2] Implication (the logical connection between the evidence and conclusion) is also known as proof. If someone has proved anything (call it B), he has pointed out some other truth (A) which is so connected to B that since A is true, B also must be true.

---

[1] In everyday discourse, where words may be used loosely and even carelessly, implication (and other words in its family: implied and implicit) sometimes means "possible suggestion" or the like. Rather, I am using the term to refer precisely to that relationship that exists among some statements such that if one is true, the other cannot be false. As Sanford says, "Implication, a relation that holds between two statements when the truth of the first ensures the truth of the second." "In ordinary discourse, 'implication' has wider meanings...." David H. Sanford, "Implication," *The Cambridge Dictionary of Philosophy*, ed. by Robert Audi (Cambridge: Cambridge University Press, 1995), p. 362.

[2] Note **logical** argument, which is argument in the good sense, a serious expression of determining truth, not argument meaning wrangling.

2

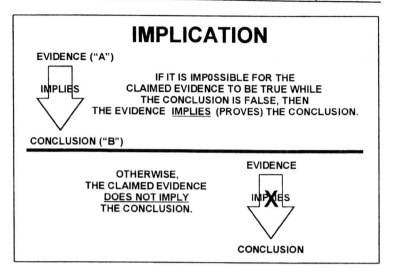

Let's look at an example of implication. John 3:16 reads, in part,

> For God so loved the world that He gave His only begotten Son...

Now let me give you a second statement:

> God so loved you that He gave His only begotten Son. (Replace "you" with your name.)

Notice that it is impossible for the first statement (Jn 3:16) to be true and for the second statement (the one with your name in it) to be false. In other words, the truthfulness of Jn 3:16 guarantees that the statement God so loved you also must be true. Or, in other words, Jn 3:16 implies that God so loved you that He gave His only begotten Son. Further, please notice that the first statement itself is in the Bible, and the second statement is not. Yet, we can know that both statements are true.[3]

---

[3] Right here is where some folks are mistaken: Some are teaching we cannot know (or even if we can know, we must not bind) statements like the second. This is the case, they continue, because such statements are "polluted by human reasoning."

Here is another example of implication. Rev 21:8 reads, in part,

> But ... all liars shall have their part in the lake which burns with fire ...."

And 2 Cor 7:10 says,

> For godly sorrow produces repentance *leading* to salvation ....

Now, observe this statement:

> A person today who continues in lying, and does not repent of it, shall be in the lake that burns with fire.

Notice that the two Bible passages taken together imply that this statement is also true. And notice that this statement is binding on us. It is binding in that being truth taught by God's word, it requires **us** today either never to lie or, if we do, to repent of the lying. But the basis of the binding is not the fact that we deduce it. It is the fact that God implied it by providing us with Rev 21:8 and 2 Cor 7:10. Our deducing it is the means we employ as the beings He created. He gave us this means and expects us to employ it to "see" and apply His Word to our lives. Why would we suppose He gave us His Word if we were not to engage in such an exercise? One is reminded of passages like Isa 55:11[4] and 2 Tim 2:15[5].

And here is a third example of implication. The Scriptures teach that, before his incarnation, Christ was in heaven with the Father:

> [1]In the beginning was the Word, and the Word was with God, and the Word was God. [2]He was

---

[4] Isa 55:11 "So shall My word be that goes forth from My mouth; It shall not return to Me void, But it shall prosper in the thing for which I sent it."
[5] 2 Tim 2:15 "Be diligent to present yourself approved to God, a worker who does not need to be ashamed, rightly dividing the word of truth."

in the beginning with God. [14]And the Word became flesh and dwelt among us, ... (Jn 1:1-2, 14)

[5]Let this mind be in you which was also in Christ Jesus, [6]who, being in the form of God, did not consider it robbery to be equal with God, [7]but made Himself of no reputation, taking the form of a bondservant, *and* coming in the likeness of men. (Phil 2:5-7)

Also, the Scriptures use the language "ascending" for going back to where the Father is, and teaches that Christ did this:

[9]Now when He had spoken these things, while they watched, He was taken up, and a cloud received Him out of their sight. [10]And while they looked steadfastly toward heaven as He went up, behold, two men stood by them in white apparel, [11]who also said, "Men of Galilee, why do you stand gazing up into heaven? This *same* Jesus, who was taken up from you into heaven, will so come in like manner as you saw Him go into heaven. (Acts 1:9-11)

So, since the Scriptures teach that (1) Christ was with the Father before the incarnation, and (2) that He **ascended**, then, using consistent language, it must be that (3) He **descended** in between these two events. That is, it is impossible for (1) and (2) to be true, and for (3) to be false. Put another way, (1) and (2) combined imply (3).

Now notice how the Holy Spirit through Paul expects us to see implication from these same events:

[9](Now this, 'He ascended'—what does it mean but that He also first descended into the lower

parts of the earth? [10]He who descended is also the One who ascended far above all the heavens, ...) Eph 4:9-10.

Examples of No Implication

Now let us illustrate a case where there is no implication. Acts 2:4 reads,

> And they were all filled with the Holy Spirit, and began to speak with other tongues, as the Spirit gave them utterance.

And observe this other statement:

> They are full of new wine. (Acts 2:13)

Here, it is not the case that the first statement guarantees the second. So those mentioned in Acts 2 who claimed the "speaking with other tongues" of the first statement as proof of the second statement are mistaken.

Here is a second example where there is no implication. Jn 4:24 reads,

> God *is* Spirit, and those who worship Him must worship in spirit and truth.

A second statement is,

> *Mr. Jackson shouldn't drive 90 MPH while driving on I-94 in Romulus, Michigan.*

If someone were to attempt to bind the second statement on Mr. Jackson and cite Jn 4:24, he would be mistaken. The italicized statement may or may not be true, but we will never know it from this Biblical passage. (For an example passage which is relevant, see Rom 13.)

So, what is implication? What does it mean to say that one statement implies another? Statement A implies statement B when it is impossible for statement A to be true *and* for statement B to be false. If this guaranteed connection is not there, there is no implication. I heard a preacher express error on this the other day on the radio. He was talking about a passage in Genesis and said that it "solidly implies that, though not with certainty." He is revealing he does not understand what implication is. Necessity, guarantee, certain linkage, is built into implication.

Explicit and Implicit

To help drive the point home, let me repeat some of what I just said, but in different words. Let's talk about *explicit* and *implicit*. Everything the Bible teaches it teaches either explicitly or implicitly. An *explicit* statement or teaching of the Bible is the very words which are actually used in the Bible. For example, 1 Tim 2:3-4 employs the very words, "God ... who desires all men to be saved." Thus, we can say that this passage explicitly teaches that "God wants all men to be saved." Notice we are using the very words which occur in the passage.

An *implicit* statement or teaching of the Bible, as the name "implicit" suggests, is a teaching which the Bible implies. That is, it is a teaching which the reader can correctly deduce **from** the very words which **are** in the Bible. Or, put in another way, the Bible's implicit teachings are those statements which must also be true due to the truth of the Bible's explicit teachings.

Summary and Exhortation

If a person claims that the Bible teaches a particular statement (doctrine) involving human behavior, then it must be that the Bible does so explicitly, implicitly, or both ways. If a person claims that the Bible teaches the statement explicitly, then (for this claim to be true), it must be that there is a Bible passage which contains the statement word-for-word. As independent thinkers, let us look for such a passage, paying attention to the Biblical context. If such a passage is there, believe the statement. If it is not there, do not believe the statement, unless it can be shown that the Bible **implies** the statement. As independent thinkers, let us thus test every such claim which humans make (Acts 17:11[6] ; 1 Th 5:21[7]; ...).

And if a person claims that the Bible teaches the statement implicitly, then (for the claim to be true) it must be that there is one Bible passage or a combination of Bible passages which cannot be true and the claimed statement false. As independent thinkers, let us look for such a passage or combination of passages, paying attention to the Biblical context. If such a passage or passages are there, believe the statement. If not, do not believe the statement, unless it can be shown that the Bible **explicitly** teaches it. As independent thinkers, let us thus test every such claim humans make (Acts 17:11; 1 Th 5:21; ...).

If the Bible does not teach the claimed statement explicitly or implicitly, do not believe the claim.

---

[6] Acts 17:11 "These were more fair-minded than those in Thessalonica, in that they received the word with all readiness, and searched the Scriptures daily *to find out* whether these things were so."

[7] 1 Th 5:21 "Test all things; hold fast what is good." The expression "test" translates the original Greek word *dokimazo*, which often, in antiquity, refers to the process of proving precious metals in a furnace. Indeed, the American Standard Version begins this passage, "Prove all things, ..." Thayer defines this Greek word as, "to test, examine, prove, scrutinize (to see whether a thing be genuine or not), as metals." J. H. Thayer, *The New Thayer's Greek-English Lexicon of the New Testament with Index* (1889; rpt. Peabody, MA: Hendrickson Publishers, 1991), p. 154.

Chapter 2
Quotations For Critique: Woodroof

I have chosen James Woodroof's expression of the doctrine in his 1990 book, *The Church in Transition*.[8] Jim has traveled through the country teaching this material. Let us notice carefully what he says:

> If God did not allow the Jewish Christians at that time to bind on others things he himself had commanded, God is not going to allow us to bind on others conclusions we have arrived at by inference and deduction. Campbell was explicit in judging such conclusions non-binding on others who do not 'perceive the connection.' That's all this book is recommending.[9]

> Further evidence shows that we became preoccupied also with a nineteenth century rationalism borrowing from the Scottish Common Sense philosophy - a system containing much to commend, but one which, if the tail starts wagging the dog, enshrines Aristotelian logic as the know-all, end-all of

---

[8] James Woodroof, *The Church in Transition* (Searcy, AK: The Bible House, Inc., 1990)

[9] Woodroof, p. 78.

9

doctrine. This philosophy has come to full flower in recent years in certain segments of the church. But when Aristotle's logic replaces Christ's perspective, we have made a wrong turn.

But this philosophy predates the Common Sense Movement and the American Restoration movement. Eusebius tells of those who...

> ... treat the divine Scriptures recklessly and without fear. They have set aside the rule of ancient faith; and Christ they have not known. They do not endeavor to learn what the Divine Scriptures declare, but strive laboriously after any form of syllogism which may be derived to sustain their impiety. And if anyone brings before them a passage of Divine Scripture, they see whether a conjunctive or disjunctive syllogism can be made from it ... they forsake the holy writings of God to devote themselves to geometry.

It is as though we have tried to discern the divine application of the Word by merely a meticulous dissecting of the Word. But this method has brought us only mass confusion and division. It is like trying to see clearly through a telescope with one lens missing. Not only does one's perception of the Word become unclear or inverted, but one's perception of himself becomes distorted as he "trusts in himself that he is righteous and despises others."[10]

On page 23, describing a poem by John Carroll Brown, Woodroof says, "... a very thought-provoking work worthy of consideration." Woodroof provides this poem at the end of his book, on pages 181 through 210. It is titled, "A Dream of Judgment," and subtitled, "A Poem Concerning Those Who Make Laws Based on Inferences from the Silence of Scripture." As seen in the quotations below, some statements in this work go beyond the matter of the silence of the Bible to implication in general.

The poem tells of an individual who has a dream in which Jesus comes to judge the world. The poem proceeds to quote Jesus' words at the judgment, and supplies several Bible passages as footnotes. All emphases are as they appear in Woodroof's book.

> Oh wayward child, why stand you here excusing your vile stand to Me? Why stand you in the way of men that they are barred from coming in to have forgiveness of their sin? For surely **you** can plainly see that your own reas'ning is to Me worth nothing! for **what men infer** and bind is **prone to err**.[11]

---

[10] Woodroof, pp. 30-31.
[11] Woodroof, p. 185.

Don't think I'm playing games with men; **MY** laws I **plainly** speak to you. If logic mind of high degree is necessary to pursue an understanding of My word, then those less gifted must depend on others to unfold My will; and so, uncertain, they must wend their way to heav'n --or else to hell; for teachers ever human are, and **human reason prone to err!** And so, astray may lead men far.[12]

...for cannot you see that scripture twisted for to prove your cherished infr'ence only serves your human pride, which thus deserves just condemnation from above.[13]

You others do despise, and find that they are cursed with baser mind who don't with your own thoughts agree -- who can't through **reason** come to see the same conclusions in detail which you have reached.[14]

Let me now critique this doctrine: ***Do not bind implication on one another***. As I mentioned previously, I also call this *the explicit-only doctrine*.

---

[12] Woodroof, p. 188.
[13] Woodroof, p. 195.
[14] Woodroof, p. 207.

Chapter 3
Three Implied Statements
We Must Bind

If I can show that there is just one implied (deduced) statement which we must bind to be pleasing to God, then I have shown that the view held by Woodroof and those who agree with him on implication is false.[15] Actually there are many such statements. We will look at three more. Each of these is a binding truth having to do with salvation - and salvation is the very purpose for which Christ came into the world (1 Tim 1:15).

    1.   Jason Jones must stop engaging in homosexual acts to be saved.

(Note that "Jason Jones," a fictitious name, could be replaced by the name of any accountable person living today who is practicing homosexuality.) This is a binding statement which has to do with salvation. It restricts Jason Jones from practicing homosexuality (if he wants to be saved). Also, if true, it forbids (binds) brethren (and everyone else) from teaching that Jason does not have to stop the homosexual behavior to be saved. **But nowhere in the Bible is this statement itself to be**

---

[15] Of course, there is a difference between a statement(s)' implying another statement, versus our claim that we "see" it. To distinguish the two, it is sometimes said that statements imply and we infer. Note, however, that if a person infers what a statement really does imply, he is seeing the truth.

13

found. No one today is going to receive direct divine revelation on this. The truth or falsity of the statement is not self-evident.[16] There is only one way Jason or anyone else living today can determine whether this statement is true: by deducing it from the relevant Biblical evidence. But Woodroof says, "... God is not going to allow us to bind on others conclusions we have arrived at by inference and deduction." And Brown teaches us that our reasoning is worth nothing and is unreliable. If they were correct, neither Jason nor any other mortal living today could determine that he ought to apply the above statement to his life as a binding truth.

But the fact is that the truthfulness of 1 Cor 6:9-10[17] and related passages guarantee that the statement is true. In other words, such Biblical passages imply this statement to be true. Thus, Jason (and all of us) may safely **deduce** its truthfulness from 1 Cor 6:9-10 and related passages. Not only may Jason deduce it. He **must** deduce this to be pleasing to God, because his name is not in the Bible. And the fact that we can correctly deduce that the statement is a binding truth proves that the position Woodroof and others are taking on implicit statements is incorrect.

---

[16] Some statements are self-evidently true: There are no married bachelors. Some are self-evidently false: The outside dimensions of this house are less than its inside dimensions. Such statements do not require travelling from evidence to conclusion.

[17] 1 Cor 6:9-10 "Do you not know that the unrighteous will not inherit the kingdom of God? Do not be deceived. Neither fornicators, nor idolaters, nor adulterers, nor homosexuals, nor sodomites, 10 nor thieves, nor covetous, nor drunkards, nor revilers, nor extortioners will inherit the kingdom of God."

Here is a second of many such examples which we could consider:

> 2.   Megan Adams, a woman living today who was only sprinkled with water as an infant, must be immersed unto the remission of sins to be saved.

This statement, if true, binds immersion in water on Megan, and has to do with salvation. Also, if true, it forbids anyone from teaching that Megan does not have to be immersed. But the statement itself is nowhere to be found in the Scriptures. Megan, who cannot find her name anywhere in the Bible, wants to know if this statement, which does have her name in it, is true or false. How can she find out? How can we as teachers of Megan know whether the statement is true or false, so we can teach her what God wants **her** to do on this matter? Here is how. We can turn to passages like 1 Pet 3:20-21[18] and find the answer, even though the statement itself, including Megan's name, is not there.

Since it is impossible for such passages to be true *and* for the above statement to be false, then **God** by such passages implies this statement to be true. In other words, passages like 1 Pet 3:20-21, which God has provided for us in His Word, are so connected or linked to statement 2 above that such passages guarantee statement 2 is true. Seeing this (so we can live accordingly) is inference and deduction. Thus, we may

---

[18] 1 Pet 3:20-21 "...who formerly were disobedient, when once the Divine longsuffering waited in the days of Noah, while the ark was being prepared, in which a few, that is, eight souls, were saved through water. [21]There is also an antitype which now saves us—baptism (not the removal of the filth of the flesh, but the answer of a good conscience toward God), through the resurrection of Jesus Christ."

15

confidently deduce that the above statement is true and know that we are teaching God's truth when we do so, even though the statement is not an explicit Bible statement. And, since the statement is not the self-evident type, and since no one is going to receive this statement by divine revelation, deduction from the Biblical evidence, "seeing the connection," is the **only** way any of us can ever answer Megan's question correctly, and know we are resisting the incorrect answer. But Woodroof says, "... God is not going to allow us to bind on others conclusions we have arrived at by inference and deduction." And Brown teaches us that our reasoning is worth nothing and is unreliable. These teachings contradict the truth we have just established and, therefore, the teaching on inference which Woodroof and Brown endorse is false.

This time we will use for an example an **explicit** teaching in the Bible:

3. ... saves us....baptism ... (1 Pet 3:21)

How do *we* who live today know this statement is true? Its truthfulness has not been revealed by **direct** divine revelation to any of *us* living today. Its truthfulness is not self-evident. Only implication is left. We can know it is true because it is implied:

If
-God exists, and
-the Bible is the word of God, and
-the Bible teaches baptism saves
Then
-baptism saves.

In fact, we can know that all explicit statements in the Bible are true only by implication as expressed in the argument above[19] (excluding any which are the self-evident type or which are deducible from nature). Replace "baptism saves" with "doctrine x" - that is, any statement in the Bible (except the self-evident or those deduced from evidence in nature) and you will be expressing the implication which allows us to know that that explicit statement is true. But Woodroof says, "... God is not going to allow us to bind on others conclusions we have arrived at by inference and deduction." Therefore, if Woodroof were correct, no **explicit** statement in the Bible could be bound, except any which is self-evident. This would eliminate much of the Bible. But Woodroof cannot be and, therefore, is not consistent with his own statement. This brings us to the next point in this analysis.

---

[19] Credit is due to Thomas B. Warren for pointing out this argument to all of us. A philosophy professor at the University of Michigan mentioned to the class one day that there is elegance in simplicity. He was commenting on a particular logical statement which was at once true, simple and powerful. I sometimes think about that comment when I consider this elegant argument about and in harmony with the Bible to which Tom has called our attention. It is at once true, simple, powerful and of eternal significance.

Chapter 4
Everyone Must Use Implication

Notice that **Woodroof's** statement is nowhere to be found in the Bible:

> ... God is not going to allow us to bind on others conclusions we have arrived at by inference and deduction.[20]

Yet he is claiming it is true. Also, he is claiming this is binding as shown by the words "God is not going to allow." There are two kinds of binding statements: *must-do's* and *must-not-do's*. He is claiming this is a *must not do*. So Woodroof is giving us a statement he claims is true and binding even though the statement is not in the Bible. How did he arrive at this alleged knowledge? By an attempt at inference and deduction. (Actually, "inference" and "deduction" are saying the same thing twice.) Notice the "if, then" structure in which he sets the statement (although he follows a common practice of omitting "then"):

---

[20] Woodroof, p. 78.

> If <u>God did not allow the Jewish Christians at
> that time to bind on others things He Himself
> had commanded,</u> <u>God is not going to allow us
> to bind on others conclusions we have arrived
> at by inference and deduction</u>.

For discussion, I have added the single and double underlines. Woodroof is claiming that the second statement, the double-underlined one, which is his conclusion, follows from the first, the single-underlined one. In other words, he is claiming there is a logical link between the first and second statements such that if the first statement is true, the second is true. This is an attempt to employ "inference and deduction." This is a claim to perceive the connection. (Whether or not he actually is correct in claiming that the first statement implies the second is a matter we shall examine momentarily.) It is the claimed truthfulness of the first statement plus this alleged logical connection between the first and second statements which allow him allegedly to "infer and deduce" that the second statement is true. Woodroof is binding on others a conclusion he has arrived at by claimed inference and deduction. The form in which he structures his words (if, then) reveals that he himself recognizes at some level (call it the intuitive level) that implication *is* a sure means of arriving at binding truth. But then he turns around and concludes that it is not. His error is revealed in two ways: (1) His conclusion contradicts the very means by which he claims to arrive at it. (2) His conclusion contradicts the fact that some truths are indeed deduced binding truths, as I have shown with the three examples.

Note that it is not your fault or my fault that Woodroof does this. Nor is it wrong to point out that a brother is wrong, especially since this is such a far-reaching error which he is spreading about the land. It is a far-reaching error because, if it were true and if followed, we could not with God's approval bind **any** *must-do* or *must-not-do* doctrine which the Bible implies, such as those mentioned in the previous examples.

It would be a right and noble thing for our beloved brother to change on this, and for any beloved brethren who agree with him or support him to change. When wrong, change.

Second, Woodroof and those whom he quotes employ inevitable inference and deduction elsewhere in his book: "Further evidence shows that ...."[21] This claims to perceive the connection.

A discussion question asks, "What evidence do you have to support your answer ...?"[22] Here he is asking the reader about perceiving the connection.

In a "meticulous dissecting" of Rom 14, and especially verses 15 through 18, Woodroof concludes there is an implied binding truth:

> He who regards the kingdom as consisting not of food and drink but of righteousness, peace and joy in the Holy Spirit, is acceptable to God. What else could Paul mean *but* that! Does not he also, then, imply that a person who fails to view the kingdom in this way is *not* acceptable to God? Is not this necessary inference?[23]

But remember, Woodroof also teaches that "God is not going to allow us to bind on others conclusions we have arrived at by

---

[21] Woodroof, p. 30.

[22] Woodroof, p. 81.

[23] Woodroof, p. 141.

inference and deduction."[24] And in the poem which Woodroof says is "a very thought-provoking work worthy of consideration" (p. 23), Brown, who provides footnotes as alleged Biblical evidence in support of **his** statements which are not themselves in the Bible, has Jesus say: "For surely **you** can plainly see that your own reas'ning is to Me worth nothing! For **what men infer** and bind is **prone to err**."[25]

We have lost confidence (not love for them, but confidence, believability) in what these men are teaching about implication. We lose confidence when they tell us we are not to bind on others conclusions we have arrived at by inference and deduction, that such conclusions are unreliable, and then try to bind on us confidently the conclusions **they** arrive at by attempted inference and deduction. We lose confidence in their claim that deductions (proofs) are unreliable, or are not to be bound, because words from an all-knowing Being who never lies require us to engage in the reasoning process, to come and reason with him (Is 1:18)[26], to prove all things and hold fast that which is good (1 Th 5:21)[27]. We lose confidence in the doctrine of implication which they deduce and defend, when we realize that there are lots of statements not **in** the Bible whose truth or falsity we can confidently deduce **from** the Biblical evidence, and can do so from generation to generation. Out of concern, a concern which issues from our love for God, our love for them, and our love for those they might influence, we resist this error at least as privately and publicly as they are teaching it, and urge these beloved brethren to make a change.

---

[24] Woodroof, p. 78.

[25] Woodroof, p. 185.

[26] Isa 1:18 "'Come now, and let us reason together,'..."

[27] 1Th 5:21 (See page 8.)

Chapter 5
Is This Claimed Logical Connection True?

W e notice again this statement:

> If God did not allow the Jewish Christians at
> that time to bind on others things He Himself
> had commanded, God is not going to allow us
> to bind on others conclusions we have arrived
> at by inference and deduction.[28]

Woodroof is claiming that the truthfulness of the first statement proves the truthfulness of the second statement. As mentioned, this shows that he intuitively recognizes the reliability of implication. He is correct in his implicit affirmation of this point (the reliability of implication) and incorrect in his explicit denial of it in the double-underlined statement. I would now like to address two questions: **Is** the first statement true? And does the first statement in fact imply the second as he claims?

His First Statement Is True If ...

The first statement is true if the "things God had commanded" is referring to those pre-New Testament doctrines from God which were nailed to the cross, such as circumcision. That is, it is true if this clause is referring to divine revelation which divine revelation later abrogated. (It is not a true statement if the meaning of the "things God had commanded" is referring to doctrines of divine revelation which are still in force - that is, which have not been abrogated or qualified by divine revelation.) I will assume he is talking about

---

[28] Woodroof, p. 78.

doctrines like circumcision, the keeping of the Sabbath, and observing the feast days to which he alludes on his page 74. Passages like Col 2:14-17[29], Gal 3:24-25[30]and others imply (!) that this meaning of Woodroof's first statement: "If <u>God did not allow the Jewish Christians at that time to bind on others things He Himself had commanded,…</u>" (which itself is not in the Bible) is true. We can know it is true because the sound argument mentioned on pages 16-17 shows that these Biblical passages are true. And these explicit statements in the Bible are logically connected to this statement in such a way that they cannot be true *and* this statement be false.

But His First Statement
Does Not Imply His Second

Although this meaning of his first statement is true, it does not imply his second statement, contrary to Woodroof's claim. That is, his first statement is not so related to the second that its truthfulness guarantees the second is true. All that need be done to show that this is the case is to show that the first statement is true and the second is false. This I have already done. So, the first statement is not logically connected to the second in such a way that the truthfulness of the first guarantees the truthfulness of the second. Thus, Woodroof is in error on this connection which he alleges, and the error is serious.

---

[29] Col 2:14-17 "having wiped out the handwriting of requirements that was against us, which was contrary to us. And He has taken it out of the way, having nailed it to the cross. [15] Having disarmed principalities and powers, He made a public spectacle of them, triumphing over them in it. [16] So let no one judge you in food or in drink, or regarding a festival or a new moon or sabbaths. [17] which are a shadow of things to come, but the substance is of Christ."

[30] Gal 3:24-25 "Therefore the law was our tutor to bring us to Christ, that we might be justified by faith. [25] But after faith has come, we are no longer under a tutor."

Chapter 6
Do Aristotle's Syllogisms Conflict with the Lord?

Woodroof deduces the following about deducing:

> Further evidence shows that we became
> preoccupied also with a nineteenth century
> rationalism borrowing from the Scottish
> Common Sense philosophy--a system
> containing much to commend, but one which,
> if the tail starts wagging the dog, enshrines
> Aristotelian logic as the know-all, end-all of
> doctrine. This philosophy has come to full
> flower in recent years in certain segments of the
> church. But when Aristotle's logic replaces
> Christ's perspective, we have made a wrong
> turn.[31]

This is atrocious reasoning. (I feel bad having to say this, but, frankly, the implications of this error make it important that it be labeled for what it is. Woodroof and the brethren who agree with him or support him, we love you. But you are promoting a serious error which must be resisted.) Again, his conclusions contradict the very means he himself employs to arrive at them. I have added italicized words amidst his words to mark where he himself attempts to employ deduction:

---

[31] Woodroof, p. 30.

24

Further evidence shows *(that is, I claim there is evidence from which I deduce)* that we became preoccupied also with a nineteenth century rationalism borrowing from the Scottish Common Sense philosophy - a system *(I conclude from other evidence)* containing much to commend, but *(I again conclude)* one which, if the tail starts wagging the dog, *(then it follows that it)* enshrines Aristotelian logic as the know-all, end-all of doctrine. This philosophy has come to full flower in recent years in certain segments of the church *(evidence allows me to deduce)*. But when Aristotle's logic replaces Christ's perspective, *(then, as can be expressed in a logical form which Aristotle named, I conclude that)* we have made a wrong turn.

The statement affirms that there can be a conflict between "Aristotelian logic" and "Christ's perspective." But "Aristotelian logic" is merely the logical relationships which exist among classes of things, which we will illustrate in a moment. Aristotle recognized that these relationships can be expressed in a three-line structure, which he called a syllogism. He recognized that there are different kinds of such relationships among classes of things, and he gave these relationships, these syllogisms, names. Aristotle is guilty of putting labels on some of the logical relationships which exist in God's reality. He is guilty of labeling a fraction of what is in mind in the wider span of logic referenced and commanded in 1 Th 5:21 - prove all things. The names he used have become traditional tags for these relationships.

There **is indeed** a problem with any view of logic which claims that using it **without the evidence revealed by divine revelation** one can determine all of God's will today, such as the plan of salvation (2 Tim 3:15-17[32]; Dt 29:29[33]; Jer 10:23[34]). But once we have that evidence, and we do in the Bible, we **must** deduce conclusions from this evidence in order to apply the Bible's words to our own lives (2 Tim 3:15-17 and 1 Th 5:21[35]).

If the "segment of the church" to which Woodroof refers is the brethren I think he means, Woodroof has missed the mark. These brethren are not denying the need for divine revelation. To the contrary, they are pointing us to passages such as 1 Th 5:21 and 1 Pet 3:15[36] which instruct us to employ proper reasoning. Divine revelation instructs us all to draw conclusions from divine revelation to our lives, so we can please God and go to heaven.

---

[32] 2 Tim 3:15-17 "and that from childhood you have known the Holy Scriptures, which are able to make you wise for salvation through faith which is in Christ Jesus. [16] All Scripture *is* given by inspiration of God, and *is* profitable for doctrine, for reproof, for correction, for instruction in righteousness. [17] that the man of God may be complete, thoroughly equipped for every good work."

[33] Dt 29:29 "'The secret *things belong* to the Lord our God, but *those things which are* revealed *belong* to us and to our children forever, that *we* may do all the words of this law."

[34] Jer 10:23 "O Lord, I know the way of man *is* not in himself; It *is* not in man who walks to direct his own steps."

[35] 1 Th 5:21 (See page 8.)

[36] 1 Pet 3:15 "But sanctify the Lord God in your hearts, and always *be* ready to *give* a defense to everyone who asks you a reason for the hope that is in you, with meekness and fear:"

26

Now, before we are persuaded by a mere claim that there is a conflict between "Aristotelian logic" and "Christ's perspective," before we become persuaded to accept this claim perhaps merely because we do not like the **sound** of the **term** "Aristotelian logic," before we become persuaded by the assumption that nothing (not anything) a Greek philosopher says could possibly be in harmony with the Bible, let us illustrate what Aristotelian logic includes. Then we can see better if we should not use some or all of it, or consider it unreliable.

As pointed out already, Aristotle noticed there are relationships between class inclusion and class exclusion. He saw there are such relationships among all, not all, some, and not some. Here is an example of such class relationships to whose form we could attach a label Aristotle gave it:

> All human beings are loved by God.
> Jennifer is a human being.
> Therefore, Jennifer is loved by God.

Behold! There **are** these relationships between such statements!! If the first two statements are true, the conclusion **does** have to be true. And what a blessed truth it is.

These relationships regarding class inclusion and class exclusion, expressed in three lines, are the types of logical relationships included in "Aristotelian logic." There is nothing wrong with these. They express truth.

Let us be critical about fatal error, not about truth and expressions of it. And let us **commend** and **promote** those who follow 1 Th 5:21, "Prove all things, hold fast that which is good." (ASV)

27

Chapter 7
More Quotations for
Critique: The Campbells

In chapters 7 through 9 I provide quotations from several others who have expressed the error just reviewed. To avoid unnecessary repetition, I will, with some, provide only relatively brief critiques, and leave any additional discussion for the reader to supply. Since more recent adherents of the error often quote the Campbells on this, we shall start with them.

Thomas Campbell

The first of many publications of the *Declaration and Address* occurred in 1809, attributed to Thomas Campbell. I will quote from a 1961 reprint.[36] In a word, the document's aim is unity. The *Declaration* is optimistic. It claims to identify a plan by which those considered Christians can rid themselves of division and attain the unity of which the Bible speaks. Biblical unity, of course, is a noble goal (Jn 17:20-21)[37]. The unity which any person advocates must comply with the Bible or it is not noble. Further, the means advocated as to how to attain this unity must be Biblical. Let us examine Campbell's words.

---

[36] *Declaration and Address and Last Will and Testament of the Springfield Presbytery* (St. Louis, MO: The Bethany Press, 1960). Page 7 of this publication, under Preface, are these words: "The corrected text of the *Declaration and Address* is used. It appeared thus in *Alexander Campbell's Memoirs of Elder Thomas Campbell* (Cincinnati: H. S. Bosworth, 1861) ...."

[37] Jn 17:20-21 [20] "I do not pray for these alone, but also for those who will believe in Me through their word; [21] "that they all may be one, as You, Father, *are* in Me, and I in You; that they also may be one in Us, that the world may believe that You sent Me.

28

The following quotation is from the *Declaration*:

...tired and sick of the bitter jarrings and janglings of a party
spirit, we would desire to be at rest; and, were it possible, we
would also desire to adopt and recommend such measures as
would give rest to our brethren throughout all the churches:
as would restore unity, peace, and purity to the whole
Church of God. This desirable rest, however, we utterly
despair either to find for ourselves, or to be able to
recommend to our brethren, by continuing amid the diversity
and rancor of party contentions, the veering uncertainty and
clashings of human opinions: nor, indeed, can we reasonably
expect to find it anywhere but in Christ and his simple word,
which is the same yesterday, to-day, and forever. Our desire,
therefore, for ourselves and our brethren would be, that,
rejecting human opinions and the inventions of men as of any
authority, or as having any place in the Church of God, we
might forever cease from further contentions about such
things; returning to and holding fast by the original standard;
taking the Divine word alone for our rule; the Holy Spirit for
our teacher and guide, to lead us into all truth; and Christ
alone, as exhibited in the word, for our salvation; that, by so
doing, we may be at peace among ourselves, follow peace
with all men, and holiness, without which no man shall see
the Lord.[38]

The cause that we advocate is not our own peculiar cause,
nor the cause of any party, considered as such; it is a
common cause, the cause of Christ and our brethren of all
denominations.[39]

The unity in mind here is broader than Biblical unity because, in
the first place, it includes as Christians those who have not even
followed the Bible teaching on how to become Christians. Further, the

---

[38] *Declaration*, p. 24.
[39] *Declaration*, p. 34.

Declaration advises that the false *explicit-only* doctrine be used as the means of attaining the unity. This is seen at least in the following quotations.

> But this we do sincerely declare, that there is nothing we have hitherto received as matter of faith or practice which is not expressly taught and enjoined in the word of God, either in express terms or approved precedent, that we would not heartily relinquish, that so we might return to the original constitutional unity of the Christian Church; and, in this happy unity, enjoy full communion with all our brethren, in peace and charity.[40]

Notice the use of the term "expressly." This is a synonym of *explicitly*. Now, Thomas Campbell gives 13 propositions for attaining the above-mentioned unity. Observe numbers 6 and 7:

> 6. That although inferences and deductions from Scripture premises, when fairly inferred, may be truly called the doctrine of God's holy word, yet are they not formally binding upon the consciences of Christians farther than they perceive the connection, and evidently see that they are so; for their faith must not stand in the wisdom of men, but in the power and veracity of God. Therefore, no such deductions can be made terms of communion, but do properly belong to the after and progressive edification of the Church. Hence, it is evident that no such deductions or inferential truths ought to have any place in the Church's confession.[41]

> 7. That although doctrinal exhibitions of the great system of Divine truths, and defensive testimonies in opposition to prevailing errors, be highly expedient, and the more full and explicit they be for those purposes, the better; yet, as these must be in a great measure the effect of human reasoning, and of course must contain many inferential truths, they ought not

---

[40] *Declaration*, p. 35.
[41] *Declaration*, p. 46. On "farther than they see the connection," see my comments on p. 239.

to be made terms of Christian communion; unless we suppose, what is contrary to fact, that none have a right to the communion of the Church, but such as possess a very clear and decisive judgment, or are come to a very high degree of doctrinal information; whereas the Church from the beginning did, and ever will, consist of little children and young men, as well as fathers.[42]

Finally, there is this last quotation found later in his book which is relevant to our analysis:

As to creeds and confessions, although we may appear to our brethren to oppose them, yet this is to be understood only in *so far* as they oppose the unity of the Church, by containing sentiments not expressly revealed in the word of God; or, by the way of using them, become the instruments of a human or implicit faith, or oppress the weak of God's heritage. Where they are liable to none of those objections, we have nothing against them.[43]

If you look carefully at these quotations you will see several planks in a proposed platform for unity. But these do not constitute a consistent and Scriptural whole. Here are some of Campbell's planks:

1. The Bible's explicit teachings are the words of **God**.
2. When we infer correctly from the Bible's explicit teachings, we do have **God's** (implicit) teachings.
3. But when we infer correctly from the Bible's explicit teachings, we have human wisdom.
4. Let us unite on 1 above and not 2. That is, we can have the unity God wants while we differ on any or all implicit Bible teachings.

---

[42] *Declaration*, p. 46.

[43] *Declaration*, p. 59.

31

We have some warped planks here, making an unsteady platform and thus one that is not able to bear the weight of saved people. Yet, we see the new "hermeneuticists" (like Woodroof, Olbricht and others we mention in Part 1) borrow boards from Thomas Campbell, even the warped ones, for **their** unity platform. One is reminded of how the Roman Catholic Church similarly uses error from the so-called "patristic" writers.

More could be added here along the same lines we followed in the critique of Woodroof. But I will leave this for the reader. If I may make a suggestion, however, a good place to start your analysis would be to answer questions like these: Are the four items above taught in the quotes from Thomas Campbell? Is 3 consistent with 2? Is 3 Scriptural? Is 4 Scriptural? Do the Bible's explicit teachings include requirements, prohibitions and options? Do the Bible's implicit teachings include requirements, prohibitions and options? Since the words in the quotes above are not explicit Bible teachings, given what Campbell says about implicit teachings, why would one want to follow his advice for attaining unity? (That is, is he consistent?)

Alexander Campbell

Thomas Campbell's son, Alexander, expresses the *explicit-only* doctrine in his periodical *The Christian Baptist*. Here he is discussing denominational creeds, which do indeed contain error. But Campbell, here, attributes these errors at least in part to inference and then throws out inference as a means of attaining Biblical unity. He fails to make the distinction between false inference and true inference. And, in the quotation below, he fails to grant the Biblically required attainability of the latter (1 Thes 5:21). He thus throws out the proverbial baby with the bath water. He writes:

> The inferences drawn by human understanding partake of all the defects of that understanding.... These conclusions, then, are always private property, and can never be placed upon a level with the inspired word. Subscription to them, or an acknowledgment of them, can never be rationally required as a *bond of union*.[44]

---

[44] Alexander Campbell, *The Christian Baptist*, Volume II (1827; rpt. Nashville: Gospel Advocate Company), p. 155.

Yet, on the title page to this volume, Campbell has "Prove all things: hold fast that which is good.' Paul the apostle"! And in a later publication, he wrote:

> ... for nothing can be rationally inferred from any verse in the Bible that is not in it; and whatever can be logically deduced from any sentence in the Book, is at much the revelation of God as anything clearly expressed in it.[45]

There is an important distinction which needs to be made: Statements that people claim the Bible implies which the Bible actually **does** imply (true inferences), versus statements that people claim the Bible implies which the Bible actually **does not** imply (false inferences). But in the first quote above, Alexander Campbell discards **all** inferences, where he should have discarded only false inferences.

Someone might point out that many of Campbell's statements through the years are sound and he should be commended. True. Let's affirm and perpetuate statements of Campbell or others which the Bible teaches. But let's not affirm his false statements, such as the first quote above. Our standard is God and not Thomas or Alexander Campbell. Let us not fall in with any tendency toward treating early restoration literature like the Roman Catholic Church treats the so-called patristic literature.

Now let us proceed to a sampling of more recent authors who express the *explicit-only* doctrine.

---

[45] Alexander Campbell, *Christianity Restored* or *A Connected View of the Principles and Rules by which the Living Oracles May Be Intelligibly and Certainly Interpreted:* ... (Bethany, VA: M'Vay and Ewing, 1835) , p. 69. This was reprinted as *Christianity Restored* (Ann Arbor: Old Paths Book Club, 1959)

Chapter 8
More Quotations for
Critique: Olbricht

Some claim Thomas Olbricht has been a major force behind much of the "new hermeneutic" thinking in churches of Christ. He taught at Abilene Christian University for several years before moving to Pepperdine University. His influence may be traced somewhat in his mostly autobiographical book titled *Hearing God's Voice*, subtitled *My Life with Scripture in Churches of Christ*. For ease of reference I will identify relevant quotations from Olbricht's material as quotes 1 through 5. I will focus on his teachings about logic ("inference") - his denial of its needful place and reliability in Bible study.

Quote 1

The command-example-necessary inference hermeneutic focuses on the rules (that is, rules of logic), and the results, rather than on the actions of God. It puts the cart before the horse. We are committed to the book of God, but not for its own sake, but to the God of the book. The old hermeneutic may help us discover what Christ did, or what we should do in the concrete. But why not begin with the actions of God, Christ, and the Holy Spirit?[46]

---

[46] Thomas H. Olbricht, *Hermeneutics: The Beginning Point*, pp. 11-12, a paper presented at the Ninth Annual Christian Scholars Conference, July 19-22, 1989 at Pepperdine University. A condensed version of this paper appears as two articles in

Note that by "old hermeneutic" in the fourth sentence of quote 1, Olbricht means "command-example-necessary inference hermeneutic." That this is so is seen on pages 3 and 5 of the paper. On page 5, he refers to what he believes is a "paradigm shift" in the churches of Christ to a new hermeneutic. On page 3 he writes, "The shift has concomitantly created agonizing soul searching in regard to our age old hermeneutics of command, example and inference." Then he discusses how authors and movements preceding the Campbells held to this "old hermeneutic."

Quotes 2 through 5 below are from Olbricht's book, *Hearing God's Voice.*

Quote 2

A major problem with the approach of those who wish to envision Scripture as chiefly a book of discrete data is that they miss the story line. In fact, they are not likely to be looking for one. In the most extreme devotees there may be a denial that a story line exists, or if it does, it is basically unimportant. In fact, if the skill required in interpreting Scripture lies in tracking down the story line--however faint-- these authorities are unemployed, because this is a different hermeneutical job description. Their expertise lies rather in amassing, concordance-style, volumes of data related to a topic in which they are interested, and, with uncommon cunning, locating a thread running through it which supports the doctrinal

---

Image Magazine (West Monroe, LA): "Hermeneutics: the Beginning Point (Part 1), September 1989, and Part 2, October 1989.

positions they push. This they do while all the time claiming--no doubt, sincerely,--that their conclusions are uncontaminated by the doctrines of men, since they range over such a wide territory of biblical facts. They categorize their conclusions with the famous term-- famous with us, anyway--"necessary inference." But what can these inferences be but doctrines of men, since they are the creations of adroit workmen, of those persons who conceived the generalizations to synthesize and bring to a conclusion the large body of data they compiled? Thomas Campbell recognized how inadvertent human inference may be in the *Declaration and Address* and therefore, while he does not deny its usefulness, does repudiate such conclusions as being the very word of God or as beneficial in distinguishing Christians from those who are not.

My proposal is not that inference should be rejected as a feature of biblical interpretation, but that the role of inference as we have commonly perceived it runs counter to what is appropriate when the nature of biblical materials is taken into account. Rather than inferring how data of Scripture is held together at a higher level of abstraction through our own inductive skills, we should be locating the skeletal core, the redemptive scheme evident in Scripture itself. The person we have been describing employs his own glue to hold together the facts in the Scriptures. I contend that he should leave his glue at home. It is not needed, since Scripture itself supplies the glue. The finely-tuned skills of inference should be employed instead for ascertaining how the story line in Scripture casts a long shadow over all the individual facts. The story line from the Scripture itself is the glue which holds together the discrete entities. The story line found in Scripture is not a doctrine of men. The "necessary" inference of the skilled polemicist may, in fact, be an unnecessary doctrine of men.[47]

Quote 3

Inference is, in fact, necessary, but it must debark from the story line of Scripture, not from generalizations drawn by those who ignore or are not even aware of the story line.[48]

Quote 4

Another relevant quotation is where Olbricht is talking about activities of an outreach team he says he helped start called "Good News Northeast." He writes:

These were interesting experiences in which we attempted to share God's voice in the Scriptures with people who were often unchurched and knew little about God or the Bible. We were reminded that interpretation involves the whole of life. We certainly made use of examples, but those offered were the

---

[47] Thomas H. Olbricht, *Hearing God's Voice* (Abilene, Texas: ACU Press, 1996), pp. 346-347.
[48] Olbricht, p. 353.

37

narratives containing the words and actions of Christ: enfleshed examples, not rational models from logic textbooks.[49]

Quote 5

Those who limit hermeneutics to technical questions regarding exegetical rules have set their sights far too low. They are willing to relegate hermeneutics to the nuts-and-bolts aspects of philology, history, and literary genres. But the ultimate end of the interpretation of Scripture is to come face-to-face with the living God.

In Restoration Doctrine I handed out a schematic itemization of the hermeneutics which I propose as useful for the course. The hermeneutics might best be described as global or theological, as compared with local, borrowing again from the weather forecast analogy. The itemization was as follows:

1. Locate the centers of the Scriptures: that is, God, Christ, and the Holy Spirit, so as to be familiar with how the Godhead informs specific commands, examples and observations.

2. Locate the mindset of the culture being addressed.

3. Select a section of the Scriptures which seems to speak to this contemporary context.

---

[49] Olbricht, p. 370.

4. Notice how the persons in this Scripture are addressed from the perspective of God, Christ and the Holy Spirit.

5. Employ a similar approach in bringing the Godhead to bear on the contemporary context.

6. Relate the specific action or understanding to the larger narrative of God's mighty works for his world through the Son and the Holy Spirit.

7. Undertake this interpretation as members together in the church of the living God.

This outline is abstract without the backgrounds provided by this book. This is the reason why I have felt inadequate to write a how-to-do-it book on hermeneutics. The same can happen as the result of reading this book, but perhaps the likelihood is less. I would argue, however, that the method outlined above is profoundly biblical, dependent at all stages upon the Scripture themselves, not upon "common sense" or manuals of logic. My proposal is, in fact, not particularly revolutionary. Something along these lines occurs whenever most people take up the Bible in an effort to discern God's will. A journey as long as this book may be necessary, if only to undo the effects of centuries of misfocused hermeneutics.[50]

---

[50] Olbricht, pp. 377-378.

Critique of Olbricht's Material

The hermeneutic advised in these quotations forces incredibly obvious errors on Olbricht and anyone else who endorses it. It is the lower-than-Scripture and outside-of-reality view of implication expressed in Woodroof.

First, let us look at quote 3. Here he tells us that inference is necessary in Bible study. But, he explains, inference **must** "debark" (that is, disembark like from a ship) **from** the story line of Scripture (the ship). What about using inference **to** the story line of Scripture? He is telling us it has no place there. Notice quote 1 carefully.

In quote 1 he uses the expression "rather than" and thus is drawing a contrast for us. He is drawing a contrast between the so-called old hermeneutic and new hermeneutic. More specifically, on one side he has determining the actions of God. In the words of quote 3, this is determining the story line of Scripture. In the words of quote 2, this is determining the skeletal core, the redemptive scheme evident in Scripture. **Only** on the other side does he have the employment of the rules of logic and their result. In the words of quote 3, only on the other side does he have the employment of inference. He is telling us that we should employ logic (inference) in Bible study. But this is to be done only after we have ascertained the actions of God (the story line) from Scripture. Otherwise, he says, we would have the cart before the horse.

This figure he employs (the cart and the horse figure) again repeats the point. Of course, a cart does not draw a horse. Rather, a horse draws a cart. The horse comes first, and then comes the cart: the cart stands for employing rules of logic (inference) in Bible study and the results of this. The horse stands for determining the actions of God, also known as the story line of Scripture. This is illustrated below.

40

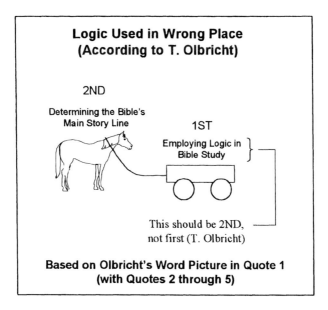

Logic Used in Wrong Place
(According to T. Olbricht)

2ND

Determining the Bible's
Main Story Line

1ST

Employing Logic in
Bible Study

This should be 2ND,
not first (T. Olbricht)

Based on Olbricht's Word Picture in Quote 1
(with Quotes 2 through 5)

So, his words now posit **two** of his conclusions before us, two obligatory rules of hermeneutics. He is giving us a *don't* and a *do,* which can be worded like this:

1. *Don't* employ rules of logic (inference) in determining the actions of God from the Bible. Another way of expressing this rule is: *Don't* employ rules of logic (inference) in determining the story line of Scripture. A third way of expressing it is: *Don't* employ rules of logic (inference) in determining the skeletal core, the redemptive scheme evident in Scripture.

2. *Do* employ rules of logic (inference) in Bible study after having determined the story line of Scripture. Or, in the words of quote 2: *Do* employ the finely tuned skills of inference for ascertaining how the story line in Scripture casts a long shadow over all the individual facts of Scripture.

The next figure illustrates his hermeneutic.

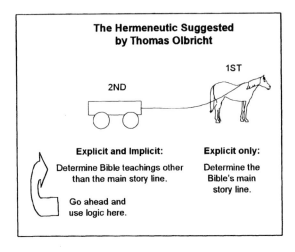

Recall the explicit-only/logic-is-unreliable claim we analyzed in Woodroof. In Olbricht, the story line of Scripture is explicit-only; and the post-story line of Scripture is implicit. The don't-use-logic-to-get-to-the-story-line rule is to prevent us from polluting this important Bible teaching (**the** story line) with human doctrine. Once we infer, we no longer have the pure teaching of God. What about the results, the conclusions, we obtain by following the do-use-logic-after-determining-the story-line rule? Well, we should not make too much of these. These are merely human. He says all of this in different ways in the quotes. For example, notice his statement toward the end of quote 2 which begins with "Thomas Campbell recognized..." "Recognized" shows that he is in agreement with his conclusions about what Campbell taught:

Thomas Campbell recognized how inadvertent human inference may be in the *Declaration and Address* and therefore, while he does not deny its usefulness, does repudiate such conclusions as being the very word of God or as beneficial in distinguishing Christians from those who are not.

42

Notice in quote 2 the disparaging language: "uncommon cunning," "their conclusions," "creations of adroit workmen," the denial that such conclusions are "uncontaminated by the doctrines of men." Compare these with Woodroof's language. For example, in Woodroof's discussion of "Aristotelian logic," he says, "It is as though we have tried to discern the divine application of the Word by merely a meticulous dissecting of the Word."[51]. Along the same line, and in violation of passages teaching us to reason with God (Is 1:18; 1 Th 5:21[52]) and to study his word (2 Tim 2:15[53]), Woodroof makes this charge: We have become "enamored by the written Word to the point of becoming oblivious to the Living Word."[54] Notice how Olbricht uses similar verbiage in quote 1: "We are committed to the book of God, but not for its own sake, but to the God of the book." Many such parallels of language can be found in the material of the new hermeneuticists.[55] This is all in connection with the false claims they are making about logic in Bible study. Do not base much on logic. Do not divide over implied Bible teachings. **Do not even use such conclusions for distinguishing between Christian and non-Christian (Olbricht's quote 2)!**

Olbricht's expressions of what I formulated as his two *don't* and *do* rules are themselves not explicit in Scripture. Further, since he did not receive these by direct divine revelation, how did he arrive at them? On what does he base them? Surely not just his say so. The only thing he has left is to attempt to infer them from

---

[51] Woodroof, p. 31.

[52] Is 1:18 (See page 21); 1 Th 5:21 (See page 8.)

[53] 2 Tim 2:15 (See page 4.) The words in this passage require us to **think** straight in all of our Bible study.

[54] Woodroof, p. 29.

[55] Note that the downplaying of the importance of all topical studies (studies sometimes termed "systematic theology") is consistent with the explicit-only doctrine.

alleged Biblical evidence. Yet, like Woodroof and Brown, his very affirmation would then be denying the means he employed to arrive at it.

Second, rules of logic must be employed many places before and during determining the actions of God in the Bible. This is so obvious it seems almost silly to explain it. For example, we have to pick out the Bible from other objects. This is going to involve proper reasoning (that is, following rules of logic), and we have not even opened the Bible yet. (We could discuss the role of implication in the translation process which happened before most Bible readers purchased their version.) Then, as we are reading the Bible to determine its main story line, we have to open it and often turn pages back and forth. Then, we will need to do some reading and sorting, concluding that from this passage I learn the story line, but from that one I cannot tell yet. From these passages together I see a theme emerging. That one, I conclude, is not dealing with the Bible's main story line. Thus finding the story line cannot be done without employing correct reasoning. Also, we have to figure out how the meanings of words in a passage relate to one another, and how the passage itself relates to context. This requires proper reasoning. The human mind does lots of this reasoning fast. But the fact that it is often done fast does not mean we are not doing it. We can show and even name the rules of logic followed in this, as well as fallacies to avoid. Further, if someone systematically expresses our reasoning in a book and uses the term "logic" somewhere in the title of that book, this does not somehow nullify the fact that we do and must employ sound logic. This is what we do when we think and we must think before and during the time we are determining what the Bible teaches, including what its main story line is.

Third, his reference to paying attention to the Bible's main story line resembles what has been pointed out for years as "Pay attention to the wider Biblical context." Notice his item 6 in quote 5.

Fourth, in quote 5 he provides us with seven items which, he claims, outline the hermeneutics he proposes. (Actually he needs to add the *do* and *don't*, resulting in at least nine.) Each starts with an imperative verb. Since none of these is an explicit Bible teaching, how did he come up with these? He is advising us to have these in mind during Bible study. The human mind which employs these rules in Bible study would have to engage in "if, then" thinking (inference). But wait. **If** I do that, **then** I would be making inferences, **seeing the connection** between Olbricht's non Bible-explicit rule(s) and the Bible itself. Further, surely, such logical moves are mentioned and explained in some logic text. One of Olbricht's hermeneutical rules is in using inference at this stage I am putting the cart before the horse. What's a Bible student to do? Give up on his doctrine about inference and determine instead to go ahead and think, and follow the divine instruction in 1 Thes 5:21 (Prove all things and hold fast to that which is good), and in Isa 1:18 (Come, let us reason together, says **JEHOVAH**)!

Fifth, look carefully at the end of quote 5. He says, "I would argue...that the method outlined...is profoundly biblical, dependent at all stages upon the Scripture themselves, not upon 'common sense' or manuals of logic." But since none of his seven items is an explicit Bible statement, then each must be the result of attempted inference (attempts at applying rules of logic which can be found in logic books). This is all he has left to arrive at the non-Bible-explicit statements in his list, which are allegedly based on the Bible. He even says this in so many words with the term **dependent** ... upon the Scripture. Then, he contradicts himself by denying this in the next

45

part of his assessment. Notice, he speaks of these as being dependent on the Scriptures; that is, he had to have arrived at these by attempted logic. But then he says they are not so based.

He has revealed the contradictory, impossible-to-follow, and thus unscriptural nature of his hermeneutic (Isa 1:18; 1 Thes 5:21; ...). He gets himself into the same problems as Woodroof and anyone who denies the need for and reality of implication in Bible study. Using Olbricht's own words, he has his own cart before his own horse. The hermeneutic, therefore, ought to be abandoned.

Chapter 9
More Quotations for Critique: Others

Michael Casey

Casey said the following in a paper delivered on July 24, 1982:

> Both Bacon and Campbell believed that only through an examination of all the evidence could the truth be found. [56]

> Campbell's scientific or inductive method of Biblical interpretation led to a pragmatic approach to scriptures that gave natural and certain conclusions. It was an approach that appealed to the common man, by arguing that any man could achieve correct interpretation of the scripture through its use.[57]

---

[56] Michael Casey, *Rhetoric of Induction: The Baconian Ideal in the Disciples Movement*, p. 4. (Presented at the Second Annual Scholars Conference, Abilene Christian University, Abilene, TX, July 24, 1982.

[57] Casey, p. 6.

47

Casey continues, saying that a lecture which J.W. McGarvey gave

> ...in his second year at the College of the Bible reveals his ideas about the inductive method. The speaker or writer was to first obtain "all the statements of scripture" on the topic by using a concordance and reading,....the speaker was to "draw from them all necessary (or logical) deductions.....[58]

Referring to the inductive method of gathering together the Biblical evidence, Casey concludes his presentation with these words:

> The churches of Christ today still face some of the problems of this approach to scriptures. We struggle with groups finding "new" teachings and methods that are seen as Biblical and others that want a scripture to authorize any practice and are quick to condemn practices that fail this test. Although it is clear the consensus on using this approach to the scriptures is weakening and other methods are developing we still reflect the values of our culture far too much in our preaching. The method of our forefathers need (*sic*) to be appreciated and understood but they should not be worshipped if we are to communicate God's word clearly to the modern world.[59]

---

[58]Casey, p. 9.
[59] Casey, p. 12.

48

Casey wrote the following in his Ph.D. dissertation at the University of Pittsburgh.[60]

> I...owe a great deal to Thomas Olbricht of Abilene Christian University for suggesting the topic and agreeing to serve on the committee.[61]

> The starting point of both the Westminster Creed and the "Cambellite" theology is the scripture and not God. The Churches of Christ emphasis on scripture is clearly derived from the Reformed tradition of Zwingli and the Westminster Creed. God does not enter the picture until Chapter two of the Westminster Creed. (One wonders sometimes where God enters the picture in "Campbellite" theology.)[62]

> The Westminster Assembly did not agree on the extent to which the practices of the primitive church were to be bound on the modern church and they recognized that some things had to be done which could not be found in the Bible.[63]

---

[60] Michael Wilson Casey, *The Development of Necessary Inference in the Hermeneutics of the Disciples of Christ/Churches of Christ* (Ann Arbor, MI: University Microfilms International, 1986)

[61] p. v (hereinafter from the dissertation).

[62] Casey, p. 24.

[63] Casey, p. 36.

Before I comment on the above, let us notice more from Casey along similar lines:

> Clearly the American Restoration Movement and its hermeneutical system owes much to the Lockean positivistic viewpoint. Thomas Olbricht correctly observed: 'The positivistic tradition is... obvious in our hermeneutic principle of commands, examples, and inferences.' The Lockean influence though is not the complete picture on how the Campbells conceptualized their hermeneutic system and theology. They both were influenced greatly by Scottish Common Sense Realism and its method of Baconian scientific induction.[64]

> Finally, it should be clear that the American Restoration hermeneutics of command, example, and later necessary inference has its origins in the eighteenth and nineteenth century philosophy of the enlightenment and not in either the Old Testament or the New.[65]

> The chief culprit was the mixing of the philosophy of John Locke with scriptural positions. Richardson saw this error as extremely insidious because it was a latent and wholly unconscious error made by most in the Restoration movement. Richardson

---

[64] Casey, pp. 53-54.
[65] Casey, p. 64.

perceptively noticed how arguments constructed for theological positions began to be mistaken for divine revelation....[66]

For the practitioner of Restoration theology in the present American Restoration tradition the most serious question this study raises is the validity of the rationalistic Restoration hermeneutic. Command, example, and necessary inference is not found in the Old or New Testament. It is grounded in the human history of Reformed theology, Scottish Common Sense philosophy and logic and the nineteenth century American culture. It is not 'divine' insulated from the 'chaos' for history. If the idea of Restoration theology is to remain viable...what should the hermeneutic be? This is the most serious challenge facing the tradition today. A failure to address this question means that the tradition is now dead, having rejected its purpose and goal.[67]

Since the Bible is the Word of God, then, by reading and applying the Bible, one is following God, not separating from Him somehow. Further, how else is one to determine God's will on a matter other than by collecting together the relevant Bible passages, drawing the conclusion which follows from them, and making the application to his life today? Why does one suppose God gave us the Bible? Does Casey and the others who deny the Biblical role of implication believe the Bible is from God? If so, then what do they advise we do with the Bible, if not go to it as thinking people, seeing the

---

[66] Casey, p. 247.
[67] Casey, p. 389.

connection between it and our lives? Serious attention needs to be given here to some very basic Biblical passages. For example, in addition to those mentioned above, see Acts 17:11[68]; 2 Tim 2:15[69]; Jas 1:21[70] and 2 Tim 3:16-17[71]....These were true in the **first** century. And their divine origin there is not nullified when human sources repeat and apply them later in history.

F. L. Lemley

In his book, *When Is An Example Binding*, Thomas B. Warren provides a few representative samples of this thinking, refutes it, and discusses the Biblical alternative to it. He points out correctly that implication is unavoidable in our determination of God's truth. He observes that, in addition to binding commands, there are Biblical statements which are not commands but, nevertheless, are binding on men living today. F. L. Lemley is one of the authors whom Warren quotes who endorses what I am calling the explicit-only doctrine.[72] Note these three quotations from Lemley which Warren provides:

> Since all inferences are of human origin, unless we want to hold on to human patterns we should discard necessary inference as poor pattern material.[73]

---

[68] Acts 17:11 "These were more fair-minded than those in Thessalonica, in that they received the word with all readiness, and searched the Scriptures daily *to find out* whether these things were so."

[69] 2 Tim 2:15 (See page 4.)

[70] Jas 1:21 "Therefore lay aside all filthiness and overflow of wickedness, and receive with meekness the implanted word, which is able to save your souls."

[71] 2 Tim 3:16-17 (See page 26.)

[72] I had the honor of assisting Tom in the development of his *You Can Understand the Bible, Volume 3: The Truth about the Truth*. See the discussion of the doctrine there also, as well as other useful information. For its availability, contact Bratton Academic Books, Inc., P.O. Box 6709, Moore, OK 73153.

[73] Quoted in Thomas B. Warren, *When Is an Example Binding?* (Jonesboro, AK: National Christian Press, 1975), P. 91. The address of the National Christian

Any time a process of human reasoning or deduction has to intervene between the word and a conclusion, the conclusion is human and not divine, and therefore cannot be (even when true) a part of the New Testament pattern.[74]

Only those examples that are the objects of direct command are binding on us.[75]

My concern with the above quotes is with the term **direct** command and with the denial of the proper role of inference. Lemley, like the others, is affirming the explicit-only doctrine. Warren points out that if the view Lemley is teaching were true, then the Bible would have to attach to every applicable command the name of every person living today. This would be needed so as to avoid that person's having to deduce that the command applies to him. He puts it like this. The Bible

would have to be directly and specifically addressed to him as a specific individual-thus his specific name would have to be used in the Bible in the giving of a specific command to him.[76]

He continues, observing that this

is one of the most absurd theories of Biblical interpretation imaginable. Since the Bible has

Press now is P.O. Box 6709, Moore, OK 73153. Lemley's article appeared in *The Firm Foundation,* July 22, 1975 (Reuel Lemmons, editor).

[74] Quoted in *When Is an Example Binding?*, p. 90. Lemley's article appeared in *The Firm Foundation,* Sept. 17, 1974 (Reuel Lemmons, editor).

[75] Qouted in *When Is an Example Binding?*, p. 91. Lemley's article appeared in *The Firm Foundation,*. July 22, 1975 (Reuel Lemmons, editor).

[76] *When Is an Example Binding?*, p. 92.

no such "direct commands" specifically directed to anyone now living, in effect, the positions noted above reject the Bible as a meaningful revelation from God to man today.[77]

Olan Hicks

Hicks wrote the following in a 1986 publication:

Some concepts are **deduced** from scripture statements which are not actually stated. Others are expressly stated. Our obligation to one is **not** the same as to the other. When we say to anyone exactly what the scripture **says** we are not making a judgment but simply repeating a judgment made by the Lord. But when we say to anyone what we **deduce as the meaning** of what the scripture says or does not say, then we are making a judgment. Concerning these opinions the Bible order is specific, **'Let Every Man Be Fully Persuaded In His Own Mind.'** The Bible never orders that concerning facts expressly stated in scripture. The difference is between **speaking as the oracles of God** and speaking as the oracles of men. Jesus was very clear on this: 'In **vain** do they worship me teaching for doctrines the commandments of men.'[78]

---

[77] p. 92.
[78] Olan Hicks, *Logic and the Gospel of Christ* (Searcy, Arkansas: Gospel Enterprises, 1986), p. 69.

54

First, many of the statements which Hicks provides in the above paragraph are not Bible-explicit. So, according to him, we need not pay much attention to these.

Second, passages like 1 Th 5:21[79] require us to hold onto implicit Bible teaching.

Third, Rom 14 (in which is found "Let every man be persuaded in his own mind") is discussing optional matters. It is not contrasting explicit versus implicit.

Fourth, one does speak the oracles of God (1 Pet 4:11[80]) when he speaks what God's word implies. For example, when one says "God loves Olan Hicks" he is speaking the oracles of God, for God himself implies this non Bible-explicit statement in Jn 3:16[81]. So God guarantees that this statement is as true as Jn 3:16 itself.

Fifth, the "doctrines of men" in Mt 15:9[82] are doctrines in conflict with God's Word, not doctrines which the explicit teachings of the Bible imply.

---

[79] 1 Th 5:21 (See page 8.)

[80] 1 Pet 4:11 "If anyone speaks, *let him speak* as the oracles of God. If anyone ministers, *let him do it* as with the ability which God supplies, that in all things God may be glorified through Jesus Christ, to whom belong the glory and the dominion forever and ever. Amen."

[81] Jn 3:16 (See page 3, text.)

[82] Mt 15:9 "And in vain they worship Me, Teaching as doctrines the commandments of men."

55

Charles Holt

Holt repeats the idea in his 1986 publication:

> One of Murphy's Laws on Technology is: 'Logic is a systematic method of coming to the wrong conclusion with confidence.' That reminds me of a number of my preaching brethren, a small hard-core group who exalt human reason and logic to the throne of worship! In fact, their faith rests in logic and their ability to use it. They apparently have little faith in anything that has not been put through the grist mill of logic. Their primary faith lies in that area. Even God's plain statements must be "rendered" as truth in their logic mill.

> They hold that the **absolute**, clear cut truth on any and every subject, pertaining to God's word, can be determined by their use of logic; you know, all those syllogisms, with major and minor premises, that produce an infallible, inerrant conclusion![83]

---

[83] Charles Holt, "Their Faith Is in Their Logic," *The Examiner* (Chattanooga, TN: Truth and Freedom Ministry, Inc., March, 1986), p. 20.

56

Randy Fenter

And Fenter puts it like this in his 1989 article:

The result of our doctrine of inference is tragic. It has resulted in a profusion of splits and factions, many of which have split again within themselves. Why has this happened? Why so many splits? It has happened because we have been so serious about what God says and does not say.[84]

David Erickson

In his 1986 article, Erickson writes:

The Campbells believed there was a 'core' or 'given' without which Christianity could not exist. For example, to talk of Christian unity in the face of denying the Incarnation would be nonsensical. But to allow a diverse interpretation or inference drawn from the Bible to interfere with fellowship would be sectarian. They believed in the distinction between what constitutes the Christian faith and that which is drawn from it by human intellect.[85]

Many a Bible student has been taught that the Word of God teaches us in three ways:

---

[84] Randy Fenter, "Do Not Go Beyond What Is Written (Part 2)," *Image Magazine* (West Monroe, LA: Worldwide Foundation, September 1989), p. 10.
[85] David Erickson, "Fact or Action," *One Body*. (Joplin, MO: One Body Ministries, Winter/Spring 1987) p. 9 ("An address delivered at the Unity Meeting in Madison, WI on April 19, 1986," says *One Body*.)

1) direct command

2) approved example, and

3) necessary inference.

This is a formula that appears to have come from the pen of Thomas Campbell in 1809, not from some remote corner of the Bible.

Unlike many who adopt his formula, Campbell recognized a descending rate of value for each type of proof. A command authorizes us to do something and, at the same time, authorizes the use of those things necessary to bring about the desired result. This is clearly the surest form of scriptural instruction and very few hermeneutic problems occur here.

A second and less certain category of instructive material is 'approved examples.' This category has generated a great deal of debate and division among God's people. ... .

The third and least certain form of instructive material is 'necessary inference.' This has also proven to be most divisive over the years. Necessary inferences are very weak evidence with which to build a theology or to be used as grounds for disassociating a brother who may disagree with our conclusions. While the concept of 'approved examples' rests heavily upon human reasoning, 'necessary inference' is wholly dependent upon it. Our past has shown us that we can have unity based upon the commands of God, but when the emphasis is on example and inference, we find ourselves lost in disunity.[86]

Dwaine Dunning

Dwaine Dunning is a member of the Christian Church who writes on this subject. In a 1983 publication, he says it like this:

> Because of inferences, logical procedures, reasonings, the Lord's Supper has become a divisive influence among Churches of Christ, rather than an unifying one. Thus the commandment of Christ has been ignored—and why? It is because those who really ought to know better than this are thinking so highly of the inferential arguments they have made that they become more important than His command, and they feel no compunction in disregarding His command![87]

> ... unity must not depend on the acceptance or rejection of logical procedures! To the degree that the mind of man enters, as it must in making inferential arguments and even in 'interpreting' precedents, to just that degree unity becomes impossible. It is hopelessly at the mercy of the weakest intellect, the most ignorant and prejudiced mind, and the most uncharitable disposition, in the group with which we may be concerned. If we allow anybody's personal views on any spiritual

---

[86] Erickson, pp. 9-10.

[87] Dwaine Dunning, *Schism by Syllogism* (published by Dwaine Dunning, 1983) p. 16.

question, we have made it inevitable that **any** man's scruples must inevitably become **every** man's fellowship concern.[88]

As we conclude Part 1, we ask "What would these folks advise us to do? Should we be logical or should we not be logical?" A man entered a bank to cash a check. The teller looked at the driver's license and said, "But this is not your picture." Complaining, the man quipped, "Oh! If you're going to use logic on me!"

Logic is not new and is not a human invention. It has been a characteristic of man since God's creation, when He made us in His image. Further, being logical, using reason, being rational, seeing implications and acting accordingly, correctly deducing, inferring what is implied, thinking straight – these distinguish a person's being in his right mind from not being in his right mind.

We remember the Babylonian King Nebuchadnezzar who eventually drew a correct conclusion about God. According to Daniel 4:33, for a while he was characterized like this:

> That very hour the word was fulfilled concerning Nebuchadnezzar; he was driven from men and ate grass like oxen; his body was wet with the dew of heaven till his hair had grown like eagles' *feathers* and his nails like bird's *claws.*

[88] Dunning, p. 17.

But according to verse 34, "... at the end of the time I, Nebuchadnezzar, lifted up my eyes to heaven, and my understanding returned to me; and I blessed and honored Him who lives forever ...." And verse 36 says, "... my reason returned to me." It is Nebuchadnezzar's **restored** condition which must characterize **us**, especially when we engage in activities of great consequence. No human activity has greater consequence than determining God's will from Bible study, and then practicing it to be heaven-bound. And there is no other way we can "cut straight"[89] (handle aright) His Word and know we are doing it, than by employing sound reasoning. May we exercise the ability He gave us to think straight. And, may we restore the practice of thinking straight about thinking straight.

---

[89] *orthotomeo* in 2 Tim 2:15.

Part 2:
Silence Forbids

There are some actions which the Bible addresses negatively, forbidding the action. An example of this is drunkenness (1 Cor 6:9-10). Simultaneously, since the Bible is consistent with itself, for such an action it never provides positive instruction, requiring it or permitting it. As we shall see, there are other actions about which the Bible has nothing to say at all: Such an action the Bible does not **address** to forbid it, to require it or to permit it - nothing. There is no passage that has to do with the particular action. There is not one thing on it in the Scriptures. What does God want us to do or not do regarding an action like this? This is the phenomenon discussed in Part 2 of this book.

Part 2 deals with three basic questions:

What does silence mean?
(Chapters 10 and 11)

What are the possible ways of interpreting silence?
(Chapter 12)

How should we interpret the **Bible's** silence?
(Chapters 13 - 20)

Chapter 10
How Silence Differs
from Implication

As we have seen, an implicit Bible teaching depends on the existence of one or more explicit Bible teachings. That is, before there can be an implicit Bible teaching there has to be something there in the Bible to do the implying. When we realize this we are well equipped to see that Bible silence is different from implication. In any body of legislation, there is silence about an action when there is nothing at all in that legislation about that action. But if one or more statements in the legislation address the action in question, explicitly or implicitly, positively or negatively, then there is something there. Then there is a passage or passages to which we can point which have to do with the action in question. And when there is something, there is not silence. Some illustrations from daily life can help us see how implication, the subject of Part 1, differs from the silence addressed in Part 2.

Let us say there are three mothers who are going away on a trip and each leaves a shopping list for her son, as well as a certain amount of money. When we look at the first list, we find the words

$\Rightarrow$ *Buy fruit.*

63

These words authorize the son to purchase apples and oranges, for example. This is the case because apples and oranges, and all other kinds of fruit, are included in the term "fruit" in this sentence ("statement"). So the statement implies that the purchase of apples and oranges is authorized. This is true, even though apples and oranges themselves are not actually named in the statement.

But there is nothing in the above statement about buying a loaf of white bread--not one thing. However, we have not read the whole list yet. The mother may very well have included a statement on the list about buying white bread. If she has, this is okay: There is no conflict between such an addition and the above statement. Further, if we discover that she has not added anything about buying white bread, this too is okay: This too does not conflict with her above statement. So, the statement *Buy fruit* allows the mother to add or not add Buy white bread, without being in logical conflict with herself. And, further, we cannot tell from this statement whether or not the mother did authorize the buying of white bread. That is, the statement, *Buy fruit* has nothing to say explicitly or implicitly, positively or negatively, about such a purchase. We cannot correctly say this at this point about the whole list, but we can at this point say this correctly about this single statement *Buy fruit*.

We continue down the list and find these additions:

> *Buy*
> $\Rightarrow$ *meat,*
> $\Rightarrow$ *white potato, and*
> $\Rightarrow$ *a box of cereal*

That's it. So we have found **nothing** in the whole list about white bread, not one thing. Thus, the first mother was **silent** about buying white bread.

64

Now we turn our attention to the second list. It says,

> *Buy*
> ⇒ *a dozen ears of corn,*
> ⇒ *a dozen tomatoes,*
> ⇒ *a loaf of bread, and*
> ⇒ *three T-bone steaks.*

This list does have something in it about buying white bread. It does not actually specify "white" bread. It just says "Buy a loaf of bread." But the statement includes the generic term "bread." It thus covers pumpernickel bread, wheat bread, white bread, and all other kinds of bread. So *Buy a loaf of bread* implies that this mother has authorized her son to buy a loaf of white bread. So there **is** something in this second list which has to do with buying a loaf of white bread. It is not the case that there is nothing in this list about it, unlike the first list. The first list is indeed silent about buying white bread. But this second list is not silent about it.

Now we look at the third list. It says,

> *Buy*
> ⇒ *one loaf of white bread,*
> ⇒ *a pound of cheese,*
> ⇒ *a dozen eggs, and*
> ⇒ *hamburger.*

This list also has something in it about buying white bread. It actually says it. So this list is not silent about such a purchase.

The second and third lists differ from the first in that they are **not** silent about buying white bread, whereas the first **is** silent about it. The second and third differ from each other merely in that the second **implicitly** covers the purchase of white bread, and the third **explicitly** covers it.

It is especially important to understand the difference between the first list and the second regarding the action in question. The point is that **implication is not an instance of silence.** Implication is not nothing. But silence is nothing. Implication can occur only when there is something there to do the implying. And in the second list there is something there which does this. Namely, the statement *Buy a loaf of bread.* Thus, this list is **not** silent about buying white bread (any more than the third list is). Only the first list is silent about it. A body of legislation is silent on an action only when there is **nothing**, **zero**, in that legislation having to do with the action in question.

We might ask, What should a person do or not do when legislation, which has jurisdiction over him, is silent about an action in question? After we define Bible silence more precisely, we will concentrate on this question. But in this chapter, and in the next, we are focusing on what silence is. This is an important first step. **Then** we can deal better with what we are to do or not do when we have silence.

Ambiguities

See the figure below. In this chapter we have illustrated two distinctions. One is that between explicit and non-explicit. The second is within the non-explicit itself, namely the distinction between implication and nothing.

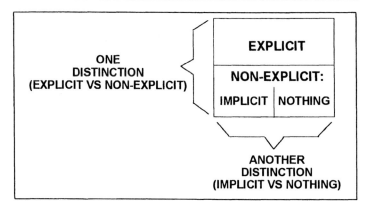

In material which discusses Bible silence, it has not been easy to find many authors who clearly explain and then clearly maintain these two distinctions throughout the discussion. This is especially the case with the second distinction. That is, some folks consider an implied Bible teaching to be an instance of Bible silence. This is a mistake.

The next illustration identifies the area on the figure which corresponds to each mother's shopping list.

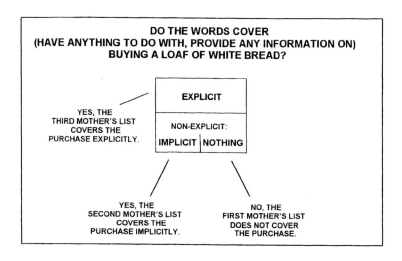

When we are listening to someone's explaining Bible silence, it is important that we ask him, early, what he means. If the answer is unclear, it could help if you point out first the difference between explicit and non-explicit. Then you could point out the difference between the two areas within the non-explicit. Then, almost there, you could ask, "Now, by Bible silence, do you mean (1) the entire non-explicit area (implicit and nothing)? Or, (2) do you mean the implicit area only? Or, (3) do you mean the nothing area only? Once you and he understand how he is defining Bible silence, then watch that both of you maintain this meaning throughout the discussion.

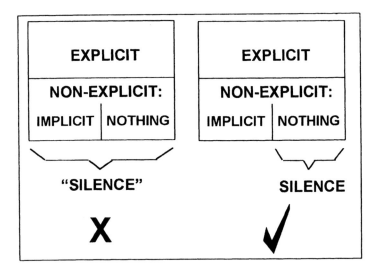

If an author equates Bible silence with the entire non-explicit area, he can easily confuse his audience and place himself in a difficult situation as he continues his discussion. Why? He then is talking about two things which are distinct from each other: implication and nothing. So he cannot now explain what we should do or not do when we have an example of Bible silence (as if he is talking about one thing.) This is the case because what he can correctly say about the nothing part of the non-explicit cannot be applied consistently to implication. Let me explain this further.

The candidate positions we often hear in discussions about Bible silence are silence permits and silence forbids. But neither of these applies consistently to implication. Let's define Bible silence as including all the non-explicit, and observe what happens. A person claims Bible silence permits. He thus claims that all implicit Bible teachings permit. This is nonsense. Some permit: *You are permitted to eat meat (Rom 14:2, 14[90])*. Some require: *You are required to love others (Mt 5:43-45[91])*. Some forbid: *You are forbidden to become drunk (1 Cor 6:9-10[92])*. (None of the foregoing italicized statements actually occurs as is in the Bible. Yet, each is proved by the indicated Bible passage. So they are implicit, not explicit, Bible teachings.) On the other hand, someone defines Bible silence as including implication, and then claims Bible silence forbids. This too is nonsense (with this wide definition of Bible silence): Not all implicit Bible teachings forbid, as just illustrated.

---

[90] Rom 14:2, 14 "[2]For one believes he may eat all things, but he who is weak eats only vegetables." "[14]I know and am convinced by the Lord Jesus that *there is* nothing unclean of itself; but to him who considers anything to be unclean, to him it *is* unclean."

[91] Mt 5:43-45 "You have heard that it was said, *'You shall love your neighbor* and hate your enemy.' 'But I say to you, love your enemies, bless those who curse you, do good to those who hate you, and pray for those who spitefully use you and persecute you. [45]that you may be sons of your Father in heaven; for He makes His sun rise on the evil and on the good, and sends rain on the just and on the unjust."

[92] 1 Cor 6:9-10 "Do you not know that the unrighteous will not inherit the kingdom of God? Do not be deceived. Neither fornicators, nor idolaters, nor adulterers, nor homosexuals, nor sodomites, [10]nor thieves, nor covetous, nor drunkards, nor revilers, nor extortioners will inherit the kingdom of God."

So, defining Bible silence as including the implicit area is not a good practice. For example, it would force one to say that the Bible is silent about whether or not God loves you or me, since your name and my name are not Bible explicit. It would also force one to say that the Bible is silent about anyone today who commits homosexuality, engages in drunkenness, murders, and so forth. In fact, including implication in the meaning of silence forces one to say that the Bible is silent about **everything** any specific individual today does, because no one today is explicitly mentioned in the Bible.

What Do You Mean by Silence?

We could present several example quotations with the aim of determining what the authors mean by Bible silence. Such an exercise would reveal the need for some to do a better job in defining Bible silence when presenting material on the subject. Let's examine what just one author says, and then spend some time discussing it.

Is the New Testament a constitution of church law, or is it a collection of epistles?

If the form of the New Testament is constitutional, then silence is intentional and necessarily prohibitive of anything not explicitly found in Scripture. Such prohibitions would include Christian colleges, schools of preaching, ownership of church property, brotherhood periodicals, radio and television programs, microphones, youth meetings, busses, bulletins, and baptisteries.

On the other hand, if Scripture is a collection of God-given, Holy Spirit-inspired letters addressed to real people with real needs, then silence is not inherently prohibitive. Silence simply means that the particular issue under discussion was not addressed in those God-given letters.[93]

I am sad to be able to say correctly that we could write a chapter in refutation of the many errors in Fenter's article. Elsewhere in his article he argues that the Bible is not a constitution and thus its silence is insignificant. The New Testament passage 2 Tim 3:16-17[94], for example, conflicts with his claim that the Bible is not a constitution. Further, he is mistaken in his view that the Bible's being constitutional implies that **all** in its non-explicit area is prohibited. Let us notice carefully how he is defining silence.

---

[93] Randy Fenter, "Do Not Go Beyond What Is Written (Part 2)," *Image Magazine* (West Monroe, LA: September 1989) p. 8.

[94] 2 Tim 3:16-17 (See page 26.) This passage teaches that the scriptures contain all good works. In other words, the Bible **is** legislative, a blueprint, a constitution. So from the scriptures one can tell what is a good work and what is not. One wonders what we are supposed to do with such instruction, if not to abide by it. So we would ask, How are the scriptures not a set of legislations? True, the scriptures are not **formed** throughout like Robert's Rules of Order or just like the United States Constitution. But this is merely a difference of form, not substance. One cannot correctly deduce from the form that therefore the Bible is not constitutional (a set of legislations for our lives guiding us to heaven out of love, a blueprint). From Biblical **narrative** in the Gospels and Acts, from **letters** like Romans, Colossians, 2 Tim and Titus one can tell what God considers acceptable behavior (good) and unacceptable behavior (sin). I invite the reader to check these and the other Bible books to find examples of how this can be determined, despite Fenter's claim the Bible is not a constitution. For starters after 2 Tim 3:16-17, you may want to consider 2 Tim 1:13, 2:15, Titus 1:9, Acts 17:11, Rom 15:9, the "must" in Jn 4:24, ...

First, notice he **is** talking about such silence forbidding *anything **not** explicitly found in Scripture.* So, he is referring to that area about which the Bible is not explicit. Also, notice he is talking about ***anything*** *not explicitly found in Scripture.* These words refer to the **entire** territory about which the Bible is not explicit. As we have mentioned,[95] the non-explicit includes two areas:

> (1) the implicit (that which the Bible implies), and

> (2) the nothing area (that which the Bible has not addressed at all, neither explicitly nor implicitly).

So the author, or at least his words, starts off with a double meaning of Bible silence. He starts off by defining Bible silence so broadly that it includes the two totally different hermeneutical phenomena in the non-explicit territory. Right here he has set himself up for some difficulty.

Second, from his examples we can tell that he is defining silence as including the implicit area. Here he gets himself into the trouble we warned about above. Look at some of his examples. Notice he lists radio and television. These means of communication are not explicit in the Bible. But there is **implied** authority for their use. The instruction "preach the Gospel to every creature" in Mk 16:15-16 implies some means of implementing it. Radio is a means. The instruction about providing for our own in 1 Tim 5:8 implies some means of implementing it. Repairing computers is a means. The instruction to assemble in Heb 10:25 requires some place to do it. Either rented grass or a purchased building is some place.

---

[95] You may find it helpful to refer back to the figures on page 67.

72

The instruction to partake of the fruit of the vine in 1 Cor 11:25 requires and thus implies some variety of fruit of the vine. It also requires some kind of container due to the nature of liquids, that the fruit of the vine be at some temperature, and that we be some place when we drink it. Fruit of the vine at 56 degrees F, occupying a tablespoon's volume in a modern container, consumed in a church building at 11:37 Sunday morning with the electric lights on so we can see, constitutes an instance of carrying out the Scriptural requirement. Only those specifics of a requirement which Scripture excludes are excluded. For example, consuming fruit of the vine that results in drunkenness is excluded by 1 Cor 6:9-10.

Do we not see, then, the importance of defining just what we mean by Bible silence when discussing it? And do we not see the difficulties we face when we define Bible silence in such a way that we include implied Bible teachings? In this book, **by Bible silence I am referring only to the nothing area of the non-explicit**. I do not include implication in the term silence. For my discussion about implication, and whether or not it is binding, I refer the reader to Part 1. In Part 2, I focus on Bible silence. It is now time to define this precisely.

Chapter 11
A Precise Definition
of Silence

We are talking about what can be termed *legislative silence* pertaining to human actions. We are not talking about some other meaning such as auditory silence (no sound heard), although there are similarities. The silence of the Bible is an instance of legislative silence. Any body of legislation can be silent about an action, not just the Bible.

To begin our route toward defining silence (legislative silence) precisely, we need to discuss some related matters and then define silence in terms of these. These related matters involve the terms *explicit* and *implicit*, as well as a discussion of *the nature of every legislative statement*. So, please bear with this for just a while, and then I will provide the definition in precise language. Some of this repeats a small portion of the material found in Part 1.

Explicit Defined
First, an explicit statement or teaching of the Bible is the very words which the Bible actually uses. For example, 1 Tim 2:3-4 employs the very words "God...desires all men to be saved..." Thus, we can say that this passage explicitly teaches that "God desires all men to be saved." Notice we are using the very words which occur in the passage.

Implicit Defined

Second, an implicit statement or teaching of the Bible, as the name "implicit" suggests, is a teaching which the Bible implies. That is, it is a teaching which the reader can correctly deduce from the very words which are in the Bible. Or, put in another way, the implicit teachings of the Bible are those statements which must be true due to the truth of the explicit teachings in the Bible.

For example, from 1 Tim 2:3-4 we can deduce that the statement *God desires you to be saved* is true (replace "you" with your name), even though this statement itself, the one with your name in it, does not actually appear in the Bible. The point is that there is no way for the explicit statement which is found in 1 Tim 2:3-4 to be true and for the implied statement *God desires you to be saved*, although it is not found in the Bible, to be false.

Kinds of Legislation

Every legislative statement in the Bible having to do with a human action either forbids the action (is a must-not-do), requires the action (is a must-do) or permits the action (is a may- or may-not-do, an option). Further, the Bible teaches either explicitly or implicitly. All of this yields six possible kinds of legislation:

1. An explicit requirement
2. An implicit requirement
3. An explicit permission
4. An implicit permission
5. An explicit prohibition
6. An implicit prohibition

These exhaust all possibilities: You will find that every legislated action falls into at least one of these six. I say "at least" because it is possible a legislated action could be taught both explicitly and implicitly.

Authorized and Unauthorized Defined

An action is *authorized* by the Bible if and only if a Bible passage or combination of Bible passages either explicitly or implicitly requires or permits the action. So an action *unauthorized* by the Bible is **not** this: That is, a Bible-unauthorized action is an action that the Bible does not require and does not permit. (This is so for an *action*, our present subject. For a *teaching* (that is, a *truth*), *authorized* means there is an explicit or implicit affirmation of it in the Bible. *Unauthorized* means there is no affirmation. See this discussed further under *Heb 1:4-5* in Chapter 17.)

Silence Defined

Now, precisely put, the Bible is silent on an action when *there is no Bible passage or combination of Bible passages which explicitly or implicitly teaches that the action is forbidden (is a must-not-do), required (is a must-do) or permitted (is an option).* In this definition, there also is information defining what is meant in Chapter 10 by "addressing an action 'positively' or 'negatively." Legislation positively addresses an action when the legislation either explicitly or implicitly requires or permits the action. Legislation negatively addresses an action when the legislation either explicitly or implicitly forbids the action.

How Unauthorized and Silence Differ

Notice that there is a difference between saying "The Bible does not authorize this action" versus saying "The Bible is silent on this action." The Bible is consistent, because it is the Word of a being who knows all and never lies. When providing information to us in Philippians, God does not forget any detail He tells us in Romans. So, if the Bible addresses an action to forbid it (explicitly or implicitly), then you will not be able to find a passage that requires or permits that action (in the same covenant arrangement, of course). Thus, if the Bible forbids an action, that action is unauthorized. So Bible-unauthorized actions include Bible-addressed prohibitions. Yet, the Bible is not silent about such an action. For example, drunkenness is forbidden in 1 Cor 6:9-10. So drunkenness is unauthorized and yet the Bible is not silent about it. If you can point to a passage or passages that forbid an action, then you have shown that the Bible is not silent about that action.

On the other hand, if the Bible **is** silent about an action, then it is also true that the Bible does not authorize that action: You will not be able to find a passage dealing with the action at all, neither forbidding it, nor requiring it, nor permitting it. (Otherwise, there is not silence.)

So, Bible-unauthorized actions is a larger category than Bible-silent actions. Bible-unauthorized actions include all those actions which the Bible addresses to forbid plus all Bible-silent actions. We can express the difference like this: *All Bible-silent actions are Bible-unauthorized actions. But not all Bible-unauthorized actions are Bible-silent actions.* It is also true that *all Bible-addressed prohibitions are Bible-unauthorized actions. But not all Bible-unauthorized actions are Bible-addressed prohibitions.* The figure below illustrates these differences.

We can express these differences in terms of the six kinds of legislation already pointed out in this chapter. If you are dealing with a Bible-addressed prohibition, then you have either an explicit prohibition or an implicit prohibition (or it is addressed both ways in the Bible). But if you are dealing with a Bible-silent action, then you have no passage categorizing the particular action as one of the six kinds of legislation. In this case, you must find out what the Bible teaches about silence to have any hope of finding out whether you may engage in that action with God's approval.

These differences are important and relevant to our study of silence. Especially important is the fact that Bible-silent actions are a subset of Bible-unauthorized actions. This means that if you can find a Bible passage that teaches that actions not authorized by God are forbidden, then you have shown that Bible-silent actions are forbidden.

The subject of Part 2 is silence as defined in this chapter. When there is silence (that is, when there is **nothing** in the legislation about an action), what are we to do or not do? The truth has to be one of four possibilities. That is, there are four possible ways of interpreting silence, as explained in the next chapter.

Chapter 12
The Possible Ways
of Interpreting Silence

I used to live in Massachusetts. At that time, after stopping at a red traffic light, it was okay for a driver to make a right turn, if a sign or authorized spokesman informed him it is okay. Silence (no sign) meant the action was **forbidden**. We knew how to interpret such silence because elsewhere in the Massachusetts system we were informed to interpret it this way.

By the time I moved to Michigan, things had changed. Now, after stopping at a red traffic light, it is okay for a driver to make a right turn, unless a sign or authorized spokesman informs him it is not okay. In this case, silence (no sign) means the action is **permitted**. Again, we know how to interpret such silence because elsewhere in the Michigan system we are informed to interpret it this way.

We can conceive of a third and a fourth possibility of interpreting silence. A third is the case in which silence **requires** an action. I do not know of a state which does this, but it is a possibility. Extending our example, a driver stops at a red light. There is no sign. This requires that he make the right turn. In such a situation, this meaning of silence would cause a problem when there is oncoming traffic, which also has authority to proceed! But we must admit the possibility that an authoritative system could inform us to interpret its silence this way, and legislate other laws which are in harmony with this for the safety of the citizenry.

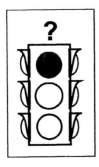

The only other possibility is the case in which a driver has **no way of determining** whether it is legal or illegal to make a right turn when there is no sign. There are no convincing clues. The authorities of the state never bothered to inform drivers in its system of laws about how to interpret its silence in such a situation. True, sometimes there are factors to consider other than what is written down somewhere. For example, regarding a left turn into oncoming traffic, the safety factor would give us a clue about what the law is or what authorities should want to make it. Sometimes, in human systems, we might wait for a judge or other authority to retroject back what he thinks we should have known. But there is the possibility that he could be unfair, though he might have good intentions. Of course, in a divine system, which provides everything for life and godliness (2 Pet 1:3), there would be no unfairness or imperfections. But returning to the case at hand, in a particular state, after a driver stops at a traffic light, we must admit the possibility that a driver would have no way of determining whether or not it is legal to make the right turn. In this case, how to interpret the silence would be unknown. We are left in the dark.

80

So, either *silence permits*, *silence forbids*, *silence requires* or *silence is unclear*. Notice that, in the first three cases, silence itself is an intended means by which the state communicates its law to a driver.[96]

Now, if the New Testament is silent on some action which we could perform today, can we or can we not perform that action and be right with God? What should we teach others regarding the practice of that action? When there is silence on an action, how does God want us to behave regarding it?

(1) By such silence does God permit the action?

(2) By such silence does He forbid the action?

(3) By such silence does He require the action? Or

(4) By such silence does He leave us in the dark regarding whether we can or cannot perform the action with His approval?

We need to address each of these and will. But before we do, we need to address a claim which, if true, would make the pursuit of the question "How should we interpret the Bible's silence?" unnecessary in our lives.

---

[96] As we shall see, all of this is leading to the fact that God, in His Word, does not consider his silence to be insignificant.

Chapter 13
No Need To Interpret
the Bible's Silence?

Someone says, "These are interesting questions. But we never will need the answers, because there is no action about which the Bible is silent." "Rather," this observer continues, "the opposite is true: Every possible action is addressed in the Bible."

Of course, if there is Biblical silence **and the Bible informs us how to interpret this silence**, then, in this sense, indeed, there is no action we could perform which the Bible does not cover. But this is not our observer's meaning.

He is claiming that the meanings of the passages found in the Bible cover (address explicitly or implicitly) every possible action and, thus, there is no silence and, thus, the Bible has no need to inform us how to interpret its silence. He is claiming the Bible covers all actions without the use of silence.

He is not claiming that God chose to cover some actions in his Word and chose not to cover other actions, but tells us what we should do about those he chose not to cover. Rather, the observer noted above is denying that the silence of the Bible is an intended means by which God communicates some of his will to man.

Both methods (covering all actions without silence and covering all actions by including silence) would succeed in communicating the same legislation as well as covering all actions.

If it is true that the Bible covers all actions without the use of silence, then, indeed, we need not concern ourselves with how to interpret the silence of the Bible, because such silence would not exist. Also, this would make it unnecessary for God to inform us in his Word about how to interpret his silence, for there would be no silence to interpret. If this is the case, so be it. We should want to accept this truth and go on to other things.

But there are at least two difficulties with our observer's claim. *First*, as shown subsequently, there **are** actions in which we could engage about which the Bible is silent. *Second*, as we shall see, the Bible does inform us how to interpret its silence. Why would its Author inform us of this if there is no need whatsoever for its readers to do it? Let us look at an example of an action about which the Bible is silent.

The Lord's Supper and its practice provides grounds for helpful study in several areas, including the area we are discussing. Jesus and his disciples were at a Jewish Passover Feast when Jesus instituted the Lord's Supper (Mt 26:17-29). His Supper was to be a memorial of the suffering he would soon undergo to deliver man from the consequence of sins. Jesus identified two elements in the Lord's Supper. Bread would represent his body, and the fruit of the vine would represent his blood. Jesus explained that he would not partake of the Lord's Supper memorial with them again until that day

83

when he drinks it with them in the kingdom. Jesus became king at his ascension and is reigning on the following Pentecost (Acts 1-2). Churches of Christ were to keep the Lord's supper as a memorial (1 Cor 11:23-34[97]). We see Paul and others at Troas doing so on the first day of the week (Acts 20:7).

Let us say that some want to add white chocolate to the Lord's Supper to represent the Savior's bones, which were included in his sacrifice for all of us. Now we have three elements. Note that this practice is not removing one of the two elements, leaving just one. Nor is this substituting one element for another resulting in just two, although one of the designated elements is now missing and is replaced by the chocolate. Rather, the two designated elements, the bread and the fruit of the vine, are still included. But now there is an added element which accompanies the two which Jesus specified. Note further that the third element is not a means, like a container, which serves as an aid for the partaking of the

---

[97] 1 Cor 11:23-34 "[23]For I received from the Lord that which I also delivered to you: that the Lord Jesus on the *same* night in which He was betrayed took bread; [24] and when He had given thanks, He broke *it* and said, "Take, eat; this is My body which is broken for you; do this in remembrance of Me." [25] In the same manner *He* also *took* the cup after supper, saying, "This cup is the new covenant in My blood. This do, as often as you drink *it,* in remembrance of Me." [26] For as often as you eat this bread and drink this cup, you proclaim the Lord's death till He comes.
"[27]Therefore whoever eats this bread or drinks *this* cup of the Lord in an unworthy manner will be guilty of the body and blood of the Lord. [28] But let a man examine himself, and so let him eat of the bread and drink of the cup. [29] For he who eats and drinks in an unworthy manner eats and drinks judgment to himself, not discerning the Lord's body. [30] For this reason many *are* weak and sick among you, and many sleep. [31] For if we would judge ourselves, we would not be judged. [32] But when we are judged, we are chastened by the Lord, that we may not be condemned with the world. [33] Therefore, my brethren, when you come together to eat, wait for one another. [34] But if anyone is hungry, let him eat at home, lest you come together for judgment. And the rest I will set in order when I come."

two elements Jesus indicated. Rather, there is an added element, so that now there are three items which will be consumed.

What passage or combination of passages in the Bible deals with adding a third element to the Lord's Supper as described above? Is there such a passage other than any which informs us how to interpret the silence of the Bible? The Lord's Supper passages themselves do not have anything to say about using chocolate as a third element. They do deal with bread and the fruit of the vine. Which ones have to do with using white chocolate to represent Christ's bones? None.

There is 1 Cor 11:23-34, which forbids consuming the Lord's Supper for the purpose of filling the belly, as in a common meal. But let us say the folks are careful not to do this. The bread and/or fruit of the vine could be consumed for this purpose. But they can be consumed only as a memorial also, and these folks are careful to do this. Similarly, one could consume chocolate to fill the belly, as desert in a common meal. But, like the other two elements, chocolate need not be consumed for this purpose. Let us say these folks are careful to consume this chocolate only as a memorial of Christ's sacrifice on the cross. They make it a point to think of the body when they partake of the bread, the blood when they partake of the fruit of the vine, and the bones when they partake of the white chocolate. They make it a point to associate in their minds the bread, the blood and the bones to Christ's loving sacrifice for their sins. They point out, then, that they are not doing what 1 Cor 11:23-24 forbids: They intentionally are thinking only of the sacrifice on the cross, and not feeding their bellies.

So where does the Bible deal with this practice? Nowhere in the Bible is there a passage whose words have to do with the use of chocolate as a third element in the Lord's Supper. No passage --except any which would tell us how to interpret the Bible's silence--no passage covers this specific action itself explicitly or implicitly. There is nothing. The Bible is thus silent on the matter. So, we have provided an example of something about which the Bible is silent.

Chapter 14
How Should We Interpret the *Bible's* Silence?

So, let us proceed. Does Bible silence leave us in the dark, require, permit or forbid?

Does Bible Silence
Leave Us in the Dark?

Some claim there is not sufficient Biblical instruction for us to know how to interpret Bible silence, and therefore we cannot tell whether God approves or disapproves the action about which the Bible is silent. What shall we say about this?

Self-Contradictory

First, some go on to claim that, since the Bible is silent on how to interpret its silence, then the Bible is neutral on what we should do or not do regarding such actions: The Bible, thus, neither forbids nor permits the action about which it is silent. So, they continue, each person may do as he himself chooses about such actions. But this amounts to saying that if Bible silence neither forbids nor permits, then it permits. Since this is self-contradictory, it is false.

2 Tim 3:16-17

Second, every system of authority, to be complete, must inform us about how to interpret its silence. Otherwise, it would not be complete, for it would be leaving us without direction on those actions about which it has nothing to say. Does the Bible claim to be complete? Yes, 2 Tim 3:16-17 speaks of Scripture as being an all-sufficient system of authority from God. Notice how Scripture speaks of itself:

> [16]All Scripture *is* given by inspiration of God, and *is* profitable for doctrine, for reproof, for correction, for instruction in righteousness. [17]that the man of God may be complete, thoroughly equipped for every good work.

So, as surely as this very passage is God's word, the Scriptures constitute His complete, all-sufficient system. Thus, they cannot leave us in the dark on whether or not it is acceptable to God for us to perform an action about which they are silent. The Bible cannot not inform us about how to interpret its silence and be true to its own claim in 2 Tim 3:16-17. Therefore, we can safely say, without fear of contradiction, that somewhere in the Bible a passage or combination of passages informs us how to interpret its silence.

Rom 14:23

Third, if there were no passage which addresses how to interpret the Bible's silence, then the Rom 14:23 principle would direct us to abstain from those actions about which it is silent. Let us notice how this would have to be the case. Rom 14 discusses brethren who were doubters and brethren who were non-doubters. The doubters did not know whether or not it was acceptable to eat meat. The non-doubters, like the apostle Paul, were aware of God's New Testament teaching (now written down for us) that eating meat is permitted (Rom

14:2, 14, 20; Acts 10:10-15; 1 Cor 10:25; 1 Tim 4:3-4). There are instructions in Rom 14 for both the doubters and the non-doubters. Rom 14:23 is an instruction to the doubters:

> But he who doubts is condemned if he eats, because he *does* not *eat* from faith; for whatever *is* not from faith is sin.

This is the *when in doubt, don't* principle. Such a doubter who does the action is in the position of doing what, as far as he knows, could be sin. This passage forbids him from doing the action.

Let me illustrate the *when in doubt, don't* principle with an experience I had while vacationing in Ireland. I was driving on a narrow road which snaked through the beautiful countryside. The road turned to the left, then to the right, then down a hill, then up a hill. I approached another vehicle moving along very slowly. I wanted to pass but there was not a long enough stretch of road without a bend or a hill to allow me to do so and assure my own safety, as well as that of others. So I waited until I could see far enough down the road to give me the certainty I needed to pass safely. This is the Rom 14:23 principle. There is a real danger in sin. The Bible teaches that if a person is not forgiven of his sins, the consequence is severe. The Lord requires us to become NT Christians by following the Bible plan of salvation. He wants the direction of the Christian's walk to be toward Him. He wants people to live righteously in this present world as He defines it in His Word so that we can be in His righteous presence forever (Titus 2:11-13). So, we must try to be righteous and avoid being unrighteous. He wants us to examine everything carefully and hold fast to that which is good (1 Th 5:21). And when in doubt, don't (Rom 14:23).

This results in a real, inner happiness, a powerful peace with God. (See Mt 5 and Phil 4:5-9.) The Christian lifestyle, as described in the New Testament, is a careful, deliberately conservative lifestyle, therefore. Though at times this can result in burdens, these are relatively light compared with the alternative (Mt 10:28-30; 25:46). And they are not worthy to be compared with the future glory (Rom 8:18).

Now, if there is no passage in the Bible which teaches either the *silence forbids* doctrine or the *silence permits* doctrine, then honesty would compel all of us to be doubters on how to interpret the Bible's silence. So if we determined that the Bible is silent on an action and is silent on its silence, we would have to be doubters about whether or not we could do that action with God's approval. We would have to be doubters like the Rom 14 vegetarians. Nay, in a sense, worse off. There is divine revelation which correctly could lead these brethren out of their doubt. But the view we are considering claims there is no such divine revelation. So we would be fixed in our doubt. In this case, the instructions in Rom 14 to non-doubters would not apply to any of us, when we are dealing with an action about which the Bible is silent. And the instructions in Rom 14 to doubters would apply to all of us, when we are dealing with such an action. Then we doubters read Rom 14:23.

> But he who doubts is condemned if he eats, because
> he *does* not *eat* from faith; for whatever is not from
> faith is sin.

This would instruct us **not to do the action about which the Bible is silent and about which, therefore, we must be in doubt** (given the view we are considering). So, if we start off our reasoning with the view that the Bible is silent on how to interpret its silence, Rom 14:23 would lead us to the *silence forbids* doctrine anyway, not the *silence permits* doctrine. (Notice the generic "whatever" in verse 23. So this principle is not limited to vegetarianism.)

Does Bible Silence Require the Action?

I address *Bible silence requires* for completeness. I know of no one who holds to it. Further, the Bible does tell us the way to interpret its silence. This is shown subsequently. So once this is established, since God does not contradict Himself, this shows that *Bible silence requires* is false.

Silence Either Permits Or Forbids

Let us focus on the two remaining ways to interpret Bible silence: either it permits or it forbids. God could legislate either one of these without conflicting with his nature. Neither one of these legislations is inherently evil. It is not wrong for God to have chosen one over the other any more than it is wrong for a human government to choose one over the other. It cannot be neither (2 Tim 3:16-17[98]) and it cannot be both because, then, an action would be forbidden and permitted (logical conflict). It has to be one and not the other.

Meanings of Silence Forbids and Silence Permits

It is important that we understand how the meanings of silence forbids and silence permits differ from one another. Every action we could choose to do either is required by God, permitted by God or forbidden by God. Since these exhaust all possibilities, then a complete meaning of one is the negation of the rest.

---

[98] See page 88 (text).

For example, the statement *either atheism or theism* exhausts all possibilities. (Agnosticism is not a third possibility in reality, for it only reflects the perceiver's alleged inability to determine which of these two real possibilities is true.) Since these two expressions (atheism and theism) exhaust all possibilities, each can be defined correctly in terms of the negation of the other-the only possibility which remains. Thus, atheism means not theism. And theism means not atheism. These are sufficient definitions.

Now, again, since the Bible is silent on some actions, yet claims to equip us unto every good work (2 Tim 3:16-17), then we can expect it to inform us how to interpret its silence regarding whether we can or cannot do those actions with God's approval. Further, that silence either requires, permits or forbids those actions. Therefore, *silence forbids* means (equals) *the Bible does not require the action and does not permit the action.* And *silence permits* means (equals) *the Bible does not require the action and does not forbid the action.* This is important. Notice where the two views differ. *Silence forbids* rests upon the fact that the Bible does not permit the action. But *silence permits* rests upon the fact that the Bible does not forbid the action. The difference is illustrated in the next figure. So, unlike the *silence forbids* view, *silence permits* is the *but-it-doesn't-say-not* doctrine. Or, to say this completely, *silence permits* is the *but-it-doesn't-say-not-to-so-it's-okay-to-do-it* doctrine. That is, it is the view that if the Bible nowhere forbids the action, then it's okay to do that action. Carefully defining the two doctrines shows that those who deny this about silence permits are mistaken.

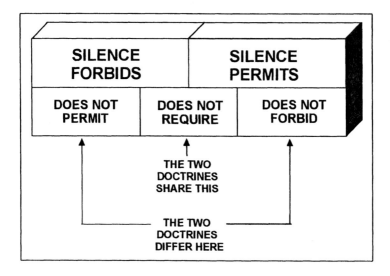

Now, which view does the Bible teach? It teaches us with several passages that its silence forbids. Let us now examine such passages.

Chapter 15
Bible Silence Forbids:
2 Tim 3:16-17
with 1 Th 5:21

The two Bible passages 2 Tim 3:16-17 and 1 Th 5:21 combine to show that the silence of the Bible forbids. The 2 Tim passage reads:

> [16]All Scripture *is* given by inspiration of God, and *is* profitable for doctrine, for reproof, for correction, for instruction in righteousness. [17]that the man of God may be complete, thoroughly equipped for every good work.

Look carefully at the last part. Notice the words "complete," "thoroughly equipped," and "every good work." It follows from this passage that if the Scriptures are silent about an action, if there is nothing in the Bible which teaches explicitly or implicitly that the action is good, then the action cannot be good. This is so because the passage claims that the Scriptures **thoroughly** equip us for every good work. Notice it does not say every work but every **good** work. And notice it is **every** good work. In this passage, then, the Scriptures speak of
94

themselves as being inclusive of all good works. So, if there is **nothing** in the Bible regarding a particular work, that is, the Bible is silent about it, then that work cannot be good.

Keep this in mind and let us now read a second passage:

> [21]Test all things; hold fast what is good.
> [22]Abstain from every form of evil.

The expression "test" translates the original Greek word *dokimazo*, which often, in antiquity, refers to the process of proving precious metals in a furnace. Thayer defines this Greek word as, "to test, examine, prove, scrutinize (to see whether a thing be genuine or not), as metals."[99] So, according to this passage, we are to determine (prove) what is good and do only it.

Now let us put the two passages together. All good works are in Scripture (2 Tim 3:16-17). So if Scripture does not address a particular work (is silent about it), then the work cannot be good. But we must **do** only what we have proved to be good (1 Th 5:21). So if we do that which is not in Scripture, where **ALL** good works are found, we violate 1 Th 5:21 and thus sin. In other words Bible silence forbids. (Observe how this underscores the importance of Bible study in our lives. Note the principle of 2 Tim 2:15, "Give diligence to present yourselves approved unto God, a workman who need not be ashamed, rightly dividing the word of truth.") Clearly, silence is an intended means by which God conveys his will to mankind.

The following figure illustrates how 2 Tim 3:16-17 with 1 Th 5:21 teach that silence forbids.

---

[99] J. H. Thayer, *The New Thayer's Greek-English Lexicon of the New Testament with Index* (1889; rpt. Peabody, MA: Hendrickson Publishers, 1981), p. 154.

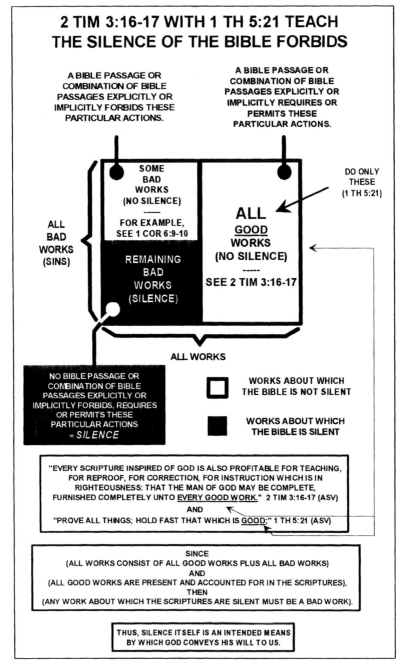

2 TIM 3:16-17 WITH 1 TH 5:21 TEACH
THE SILENCE OF THE BIBLE FORBIDS

A BIBLE PASSAGE OR COMBINATION OF BIBLE PASSAGES EXPLICITLY OR IMPLICITLY FORBIDS THESE PARTICULAR ACTIONS.

A BIBLE PASSAGE OR COMBINATION OF BIBLE PASSAGES EXPLICITLY OR IMPLICITLY REQUIRES OR PERMITS THESE PARTICULAR ACTIONS.

SOME BAD WORKS (NO SILENCE)
——
FOR EXAMPLE, SEE 1 COR 6:9-10

REMAINING BAD WORKS (SILENCE)

ALL GOOD WORKS (NO SILENCE)

SEE 2 TIM 3:16-17

DO ONLY THESE (1 TH 5:21)

ALL BAD WORKS (SINS)

ALL WORKS

NO BIBLE PASSAGE OR COMBINATION OF BIBLE PASSAGES EXPLICITLY OR IMPLICITLY FORBIDS, REQUIRES OR PERMITS THESE PARTICULAR ACTIONS = SILENCE

☐ WORKS ABOUT WHICH THE BIBLE IS NOT SILENT

■ WORKS ABOUT WHICH THE BIBLE IS SILENT

"EVERY SCRIPTURE INSPIRED OF GOD IS ALSO PROFITABLE FOR TEACHING, FOR REPROOF, FOR CORRECTION, FOR INSTRUCTION WHICH IS IN RIGHTEOUSNESS: THAT THE MAN OF GOD MAY BE COMPLETE, FURNISHED COMPLETELY UNTO EVERY GOOD WORK." 2 TIM 3:16-17 (ASV)
AND
"PROVE ALL THINGS; HOLD FAST THAT WHICH IS GOOD;" 1 TH 5:21 (ASV)

SINCE
(ALL WORKS CONSIST OF ALL GOOD WORKS PLUS ALL BAD WORKS)
AND
(ALL GOOD WORKS ARE PRESENT AND ACCOUNTED FOR IN THE SCRIPTURES),
THEN
(ANY WORK ABOUT WHICH THE SCRIPTURES ARE SILENT MUST BE A BAD WORK).

THUS, SILENCE ITSELF IS AN INTENDED MEANS BY WHICH GOD CONVEYS HIS WILL TO US.

An Objection

The Scriptures to which Paul is referring in 2 Tim 3:15-17 include the Old Testament Scriptures but cannot include all of the New Testament Scriptures.[100] Thus, the passage is not referring to the whole Bible, contrary to what you are claiming. This is shown by the following facts. The "you" to which Paul refers in verse 15 is Timothy (2 Tim 1:2). Paul is writing the letter of 2 Timothy toward the end of his life (2 Tim 4:6-8). Paul is alive at the end of the book of Acts (Acts 28). Twelve chapters earlier Paul meets with Timothy at which time Timothy was old enough to be a disciple (Acts 16:1-3). The Delphi Inscription dates Acts 18:12 at no later than 51 A.D. Now, the Sacred Writings referenced in 2 Tim 3:15 are described as those which Timothy had known "from childhood." So whatever the books are to which Paul is referring in the 2 Timothy passage they had to have been written several years before Acts 16 (well before 51 A.D.). Therefore, it is stretching things even to include **any** of the New Testament books in the Scripture referenced in 2 Tim 3:15-17. But for sure the Scriptures referenced do not include all of the New Testament books. (Note that the references to Timothy's youth, to which Paul refers in 2 Tim 2:22 and 1 Tim 4:22, could be understood relatively: Timothy is a youth relative to Paul). So then, the argument based on this passage that the Scriptures, meaning the whole Bible, include all good works is faulty.

---

[100] For example, notice Thomas Olbricht's claim: After quoting 2 Tim 3:16-17, he writes, "That Scripture, it dawned on me, is explicitly about the Old Testament, not the New." (*Hearing God's Voice*, p. 233)

Reply

I do not base my case upon the "sacred writings" (ASV) in verse 15 but upon the "scripture" in verse 16 . It is true that the sacred writings in verse 15 are those which Timothy learned from childhood and that, as shown in the above reasoning, these could not have included the whole Bible. In fact, one would be hard pressed to show that these sacred writings in verse 15 included more than the Old Testament Scriptures. But the scripture described in verses 16 and 17 is wider in scope than those in verse 15 and must be the entire scriptures, as the following reasoning demonstrates.

First, there is no grammatical linkage at the end of verse 15 or at the beginning of verse 16 which disallows the "scripture" in verse 16 to be wider in scope than the "sacred writings" in verse 15. Though this fact does not prove that verse 16 is wider in scope than 15, it allows it to be. But let us go on further.

Second, the "scripture" in verse 16 is described in verse 17 as including "every" good work. So, if I can find one work which the New Testament teaches is good during the time Paul is writing, which is not mentioned in the Old Testament as good, then I **have** shown that the scripture in verse 16 **does** include more than the Old Testament. What about partaking of the Lord's supper? Was that a good work at the time Paul was writing? It has to be because applicable scriptures instruct us to partake of it. But the Old Testament does not instruct people to partake of the Lord's supper. So we have found a good work in the New Testament, during the time Paul wrote 2 Timothy, which is not in the Old Testament. And, since the scripture to which Paul refers in verses 16 and 17 contains **all** good works, then it is wider in scope than the Old Testament referenced in verse 15.

Next, what about believing that Jesus of Nazareth was born **as a past fact** and that He is the Messiah predicted in the Old Testament? Is that belief a good work by the time Paul is writing? Jn 6:28-29[101] teaches that it is. But such belief (that Jesus is the Messiah **and had already lived on earth**) is not a good work of the Old Testament. Therefore, the "scripture" in verse 16 is wider in scope than the sacred writings in verse 15.

Next, what about the eating of pork? During the Old Testament dispensation, eating pork was not a good work (Lev 11:7). But, during the time Paul was writing, eating pork was permitted and thus had to be good (Acts 10:15; 1 Tim 4:3). These and other examples could be given which show that, to satisfy the wording in 2 Tim 3:16-17, the scripture in mind there include more than sacred writings mentioned in verse 15.

Third, consider this thinking: Verse 16 says "every" scripture. Every means every. So the Holy Spirit is talking about every scripture. So the scripture to which Paul is referring includes more than the Old Testament Scriptures. It includes more than the sacred writings Timothy could have learned from childhood, for there is scripture from God which came after his childhood.

Another Objection

Now, someone says, "Okay. I abandon the argument that Paul is only including the Old Testament in verses 16 and 17. But aren't we now forced into saying that, at the time Paul wrote 2 Timothy, all Scripture existed? It is often claimed that 2 Tim was written about A.D. 64-66. So aren't we forced into

---

[101] Jn 6:28-29 "Then they said to Him, 'What shall we do, that we may work the works of God?' [29] Jesus answered and said to them, 'This is the work of God, that you believe in Him whom He sent.' "

saying that any and all Bible books written after 2 Timothy are not part of these complete Scriptures? Since the Scriptures in mind in verses 16 and 17 include every good work, then what is the need for any additional revelation after 2 Timothy?"

Reply

First, it is true that the passage is describing complete divinely inspired Scripture ("all", "every", "thoroughly equipped"). But God can talk about something as complete (all-sufficient) whether that thing is in the past, the present or the future. The difference here is the same as that between an adjective and a verb. Teaching that something is complete does not guarantee that it has been completed now.

What words in the passage teach that the "all scripture" was available at the time Paul wrote 2 Timothy? Saying that "all scripture is inspired of God" is not the same as saying "all scripture is inspired of God <u>and has now been finished with this letter</u>." Teaching that, by means of the Scriptures, "the man of God might be complete, thoroughly furnished unto every good work" is not the same as teaching that, by means of the Scriptures, "the man of God might be complete, thoroughly furnished unto every good work <u>and this you now have</u>." The underlined portions of the previous sentences are not in our passage. The passage does speak of all-sufficient, divinely inspired Scripture. But it does not speak of when such a blessing will be available. We will have to go elsewhere to determine this.

Second, a similar point is sometimes made regarding Jude 3,

> ...contend earnestly for the faith which was once for all delivered to the saints.

Peter used similar language:

> ...His divine power has given to us all things that *pertain* to life and godliness, through the true knowledge of Him ...." (2 Pet 1:3)

"Once for all delivered?" someone says. "Has given?" Then why was any scripture needed after Jude and 2 Peter?"

This is not a clincher because it fails to take into account the ramification of the difference between oral revelation and written revelation. Why could not the faith once for all delivered mentioned in Jude, and the everything that has been granted mentioned in 2 Peter be referring to the completed set of doctrines given orally, **before** they were deposited in Scripture? Where is "Scripture" mentioned in these passages? The following sequence is in full harmony with Biblical teaching.

While on earth, Jesus told His disciples he would send the Holy Spirit who would do two things: give them a (perfect) remembrance of what He taught, and teach more truth than what Jesus taught while on earth. This, Jesus described as "all truth." Next, the "all truth" was being delivered part-by-part through prophets over several decades of the first century. This took place in oral form, then in oral and written form, then, after all the apostles and prophets died, all that was left was the written form (gift of prophecy, etc.: 1 Cor 12:8, 10; oral and written for a while: 2 Thes 2:15). The 2 Tim 3:16-17 passage refers to the "all truth" in written form, but does not tell us it has happened. Jud 3 and 2 Pet 1:3 tell us the "all truth" has happened but does not tell us it has happened in written form.

101

What fits everything is this: The all truth having been delivered, referenced in Jude 3 and 2 Pet 1:3, is the oral form. This happened before it all was deposited in Scripture. It was after this that the faith once for all delivered (orally) was deposited in Scripture.

Finally, there is this consideration. As I have discussed, I believe 2 Tim 3:16-17 describes complete (all-sufficient) Scripture, and not Scripture that has been completed. Sometimes in the Bible a future action of God can be expressed as happening in present time, due to its certainty. Notice these two Bible examples:

> [28] "For this is My blood of the new covenant, which is shed for many for the remission of sins. (Mt 26:28)

> [5] "No longer shall your name be called Abram, but your name shall be Abraham; for I have made you a father of many nations. (Gen 17:5)

In the Matthew passage, Jesus speaks of His blood of the NT "which is shed", even though He was not yet on the cross. But it was certain. So He spoke of it as if it were already present. Similarly, in the Genesis passage, God said to Abram "I have made you a father of many nations" though it had not yet occurred.[102]

---

[102] Thanks to William Woodson for pointing out these two examples when reviewing the draft of this book.

Chapter 16
Bible Silence Forbids:
Col 3:17

Col 3:17 reads:

And *whatever*[103] you do in word or deed, *do* all
in the name of the Lord Jesus, giving thanks to
God the Father through Him.

First, notice the passage is referring to **everything** we do.
It tells us this three times: (1) by the term "**whatever** you do,"
(2) by the all-inclusive term "**in word or deed**," and (3), in case
we still do not see it, by the term "do **all**." So the passage is
talking about everything we do.

---

[103] The publisher of the NKJV, Thomas Nelson, Inc., is mistaken in italicizing
"whatever" in this verse. Italics indicates supplied text, according to their
preface: "Words or phrases in *italics* indicate expressions in the original
language which require clarification by additional English words, as also done
throughout the history of the King James Bible." But there **is** a Greek term
behind the "whatever." (The construction Paul uses that is cited in the Nestle-
Aland[26] Greek text piles up words that cover the widest range of activity: *pan
(every thing) ho (which thing) ti (something, whatever thing) ean poiete (if you
might do):* "everything whatever which you might do," or "whatever you do."
Some Greek texts combine the *ho* and *ti* into the one word *hoti*, "that." But
still the widest range of activity is retained in *pan*.) The publisher correctly,
though inconsistently, uses the non-italicized "whatever" a few verses later at
1:23. In consulting the apparatus of Greek texts, I consistently saw a Greek
expression to be translated by the English "whatever" or a synonym (Nestle-
Aland, ed. 26; United Bible Society, ed. 4). The **meaning** of verse seventeen's
"whatever" is repeated by two other expressions in the verse ("in word or
deed" and "do all"). So the mistake does not lose the apostle's meaning.
Nevertheless, accuracy is best. Several years ago, I sent a letter to the
publisher explaining this in considerable detail. I have not heard from them.
We might watch for a subsequent edition of the NKJV which changes the
italics.

Second, notice the expression "in the name of the Lord Jesus." This identifies the authority in whose jurisdiction the whatever you do is to be done. "Lord" is the word used in the master-servant relationship. It is conveying the idea that Jesus is the authority. He is the master. Thus, "Lord" Jesus in this context, after talking about "do all," suggests that all is to be done by the authority of Jesus. Compare the words of Jesus in Mt 28:18, "All authority has been given to Me in heaven and on earth." Then in verse 19 of that chapter Jesus gives a directive. In addition to "Lord," the expression "in the name of" in Col 3:17 conveys authority. "In the name of" means "by the authority of." It is like saying, "Open up in the name of the law." That is, open up by the authority of the law. That "in the name of" has this meaning in Scripture becomes plain after observing the use of the word "name" in other Bible passages. For example, notice the three occurrences of "name" in this passage from the book of Acts, and notice how "name" can be replaced with the word "authority:"

> [7] ... 'By what power, or by what name, have you done this?' [8] Then Peter, filled with the Holy Spirit, said to them, 'Rulers of the people and elders of Israel:, ...' [10] 'let it be known to you all ... that by the name of Jesus Christ ... this man stands before you whole. ...' [12] 'Nor is there salvation in any other, for there is no other name under heaven given among men, by which we must be saved.' (Acts 4:7-12)

Another passage showing this is Eph 1:21-22:

> [21] far above all principality and power and might and dominion, and every name that is named, not only in this age, but also in that which is to come. [22] And He put all *things* under His feet, ..."

It is clear that "name" in this passage means "authority." Similarly Col 3:17 is teaching that everything we do must have the authority of Jesus, the master, to whom all authority has been given.

Third, where do we find Christ's authority? It is found in the New Testament Scriptures.[104] Let me overview the Biblical evidence for this. In Jn 14:26, Jesus promised the apostles that he would send the Holy Spirit, and then says,

> ...He will teach you all things, and bring to your remembrance all things that I said to you.

He repeats the essence of this in Jn 16:13:

> However when He, the Spirit of Truth, has come, He will guide you into all the truth; for He will not speak on His own *authority*, but whatever He hears, He will speak; and He will tell you things to come.

---

[104] The OT drives us to the NT. The OT looks forward to its own replacement, for example, in Jer 31:31-34.

105

Observe in these passages that Jesus says the Holy Spirit would do two things:

> (1) teach them **all** things (something, then, Jesus did not do during his earthly ministry) and
>
> (2) cause them to remember what he did teach them during his earthly ministry.

This is a promise of divine and thus perfect assistance. Notice the two occurrences of "all" in Jn 14:26. The Holy Spirit will give them a recollection of **all** that Jesus taught while he was on earth. And will reveal **all** things. Jesus thus promised to give them a complete set of teachings.

This completeness, the "all" things taught, are found in Scripture, according to another passage, which we have already discussed (2 Tim 3:16-17). It is not found in the conflicting doctrines of men. Note again this passage:

> [16]All Scripture *is* given by inspiration of God, and is profitable for doctrine, for reproof, for correction, for instruction in righteousness; [17]that the man of God may be complete, thoroughly equipped for every good work.

In the first century, Jude could speak of the finality of the faith (that is, collection of teachings). Notice Jude 3:

> ... contend earnestly for the faith which was once for all delivered to the saints.

Peter used similar language in 2 Pet 1:3:

> ... His divine power has given to us all things that *pertain* to life and godliness, through the knowledge of Him ....

Further, notice in Jn 14:26 the words, "bring to your remembrance all that I said to you." So the "you" in mind in this verse is those who were with him in the first century. Some had miraculous gifts which included the gift of prophecy. Such gifts could only be imparted through the laying on of an apostles hands. (Acts 8:14-18[105]; 1 Cor 12:1-11)[106]. All apostles have died. So now, as worked out by God, all we have are the Scriptures. These are complete (2 Tim 3:16-17). Today, we are under the New Testament (Col 2:14-17).

And so **everything** we **do** must be authorized by the New Testament. Col 3:17 contradicts the *silence permits* doctrine. This is so because, as shown in Chapter 14, the meaning of the *silence permits* doctrine includes the idea that, if the Bible does not prohibit the action (if "it doesn't say not to") it is okay to do that action. Not so according to Col 3:17. Rather, the "whatever you **do**, **do all** in the name of the Lord

---

[105] Acts 8:14-18 "Now when the apostles who were at Jerusalem heard that Samaria had received the word of God, they sent Peter and John to them, [15]who, when they had come down, prayed for them that they might receive the Holy Spirit. [16]For as yet He had fallen upon none of them. They had only been baptized in the name of the Lord Jesus. [17]Then they laid hands on them, and they received the Holy Spirit. [18]And when Simon saw that through the laying on of the apostles' hands the Holy Spirit was given, he offered them money."

[106] 1 Cor 12: 1-11 "Now concerning spiritual *gifts*, brethren, I do not want you to be ignorant: [2]You know that you were Gentiles, carried away to these dumb idols, however you were led. [3]Therefore I make known to you that no one speaking by the Spirit of God calls Jesus accursed, and no one can say that Jesus is Lord except by the Holy Spirit. [4]There are diversities of gifts, but the same Spirit. 5 There are differences of ministries, but the same Lord. [6]And there are diversities of activities, but it is the same God who works all in all. [7]But the manifestation of the Spirit is given to each one for the profit *of* all: [8]for to one is given the word of wisdom through the Spirit, to another the word of knowledge through the same Spirit, [9]to another faith by the same Spirit, to another gifts of healings by the same Spirit, [10]to another the working of miracles, to another prophecy, to another discerning of spirits, to another *different* kinds of tongues, to another the interpretation of tongues. [11]But one and the same Spirit works all these things, distributing to each one individually as He wills."

Jesus" wording of this passage teaches that we must find Christ's authority for everything we do. And since Christ's authority is found in Scripture, then, if an action is right with God, there must be a Bible passage or combination of Bible passages which explicitly or implicitly requires or permits it. If there is not such a passage (and if there is Bible silence on the action, there is not), then we cannot accomplish what Col 3:17 instructs us to accomplish for doing that action. If we go ahead and do the action anyway, when there is no passage covering it, we violate Col 3:17. And violating the word of God is sin (1 Jn 3:4).

A circle including all human actions authorized (=required or permitted) by the New Testament illustrates this. See the inner circle in the following figure. Col 3:17 teaches that everything you do has to be in this circle. But if the NT is silent about the action, then there is no New Testament passage or combination of passages which requires or permits the action. The action is outside this circle, unauthorized.[107] So you would be violating Col 3:17 if you do that action.

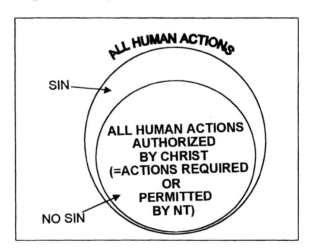

---

[107] Recall the meanings of authorized and unauthorized from Chapter 11.

Chapter 17
Bible Silence Forbids:
Passages in Hebrews

By (1) 2 Tim 3:16-17 with 1 Thes 5:21 and (2) Col 3:17 we have shown that Bible silence forbids is a NT doctrine. The NT book of Hebrews shows that the doctrine was true during the times covered by the OT Scriptures as well as NT times. This covers the time since creation, through the patriarchal age, through the Mosaic age and into our own (NT) age.

In this chapter, we will examine six passages or passage combinations:

- Heb 1:4-5

- Heb 1:13

- Heb 5:1-10

- Heb 7:20-22

- Heb 7:13-14 with 8:4-5

- Heb 13:10-11

It will prove helpful to begin with an overview of the book.

109

Overview of Hebrews

That in God's plan the OT has served its purpose and has been replaced by Christ and His NT is repeatedly taught in the book of Hebrews. Faithful men and women recorded in the OT Scriptures, from Genesis on, lived in times only anticipatory of the greater blessings now available in Christ. They did not receive the Genesis 12:3 promise, "God having provided something better for" the writer and readers of Hebrews (Heb 11:39-40).[108] The book expresses arguments one after the other to persuade its readers that this is so. Christ has come now and is superior to a covenant heretofore given. So stay with Him and do not regress by returning to a system that anticipates Him.

As we observe this theme developing in Hebrews, we see interpretations of Scriptures, a hermeneutic, that is very much to the point of our study. The book starts off with a reference to the fact that God has revealed His will progressively:

> [1]God, who at various times and in various ways spoke in time past to the fathers by the prophets, [2] has in these last days spoken to us by *His* Son, whom He has appointed heir of all things, ...

Conclusions are drawn not only on the basis of what God said, but also on the basis of what God did not say. Let's notice this in our first passage for examination.

---

[108] Heb 11:39-40 " [39]And all these, having obtained a good testimony through faith, did not receive the promise, [40] God having provided something better for us, that they should not be made perfect apart from us."

Heb 1:4-5

In its context, this passage reads,

"... when He had by Himself purged our sins, sat down at the right hand of the Majesty on high, [4]having become so much better than the angels, as He has by inheritance obtained a more excellent name than they. [5]For to which of the angels did He ever say: 'You are My Son, Today I have begotten You"? And again: 'I will be to Him a Father, And He shall be to Me a Son"? (Heb 1:3-5)

"For" at the beginning of verse 5 translates the Greek word *gar*. This word introduces a reason or explanation of what was just said.[109] The passage is giving us an argument that can be expressed like this:

Since
    (a) God's word does affirm that Christ is king, and
    (b) God's word does not affirm that any angel is king,

Then,
    Conclusion: Christ is better than angels. ("Better than" at least means "higher in authority" than [110]).

Consistent with the use of *gar*, the order above is switched: The reasons, (a) and (b), are in verse 5, and the conclusion is in verse 4.

---

[109] "... by the use of this particle, either the reason or cause of a foregoing statement is added, whence arises the causal or argumentative force of the particle, *for* ...; or some previous declaration is explained, whence *gar* takes on an explicative force: *for, the fact is, namely* ...." Joseph Henry Thayer, *The New Thayer's Greek-English Lexicon of the New Testament with Index* (1889; rpt. Peabody, MA: Hendrickson Publishers, 1981), p. 109.

[110] Notice "more excellent name than they" in verse 4: See the discussion of "name" previously given in Chapter 16.

111

Notice in the argument that the conclusion follows from the fact that **both** (a) and (b) are true. From (a) alone we can conclude that Christ is king. But just from that we cannot conclude that He is better than (in the sense of being higher in authority than) all angels, because maybe an angel also is king. However, the writer gives us (b) along with (a). Due to (a) and (b) combined he **expects** us now to view Christ as better than angels. A question to ask right here is, **According to the Bible in this passage**, why are we not to include in our belief system the doctrine that an angel is king? The answer is, Because in God's word there is **no affirmation** of it. The writer expects us to answer "None" to the question in verse 5 starting with "to which of the angels did He ever say...."

Observe in Heb 1:3-4 the words, "... sat down at the right hand of the Majesty on high, having become so much better than the angels, ..." The "having become" encompasses Christ's ascension to this throne. This is what **is** said of Christ that is **not said** of any angel. It is what we have called "(a)", found in verse 5. The quotation from Psalm 2 identifies one of the places in God's Word where this is said of Christ:[111]

^{6'}Yet I have set My King On My holy hill of Zion.' ^{7'}I will declare the decree:The LORD has said to Me, "You *are* My Son, Today I have begotten You." (Ps 2:6-7)

Christ became a Son in the sense of Ps 2 when He became king. He became king when he ascended. Compare Acts 2:29-36.[112] No such affirmation in God's Word can be found of any angel. So we are not to and do not believe it.

---

[111] The second quotation in verse 5 is from 2 Sam 7:14, which repeats the essence of the first quotation.

[112] ²⁹ "Men *and* brethren, let *me* speak freely to you of the patriarch David, that he is both dead and buried, and his tomb is with us to this day. ³⁰ "Therefore, being a prophet, and knowing that God had sworn with an oath to

We recognize this thinking when we consider how a person may and may not become king in human terms. For example, let us say the law states that on the day when the present king dies, his oldest son ascends to the throne. Now the king dies. So his oldest son Edward ascends with the attendant ceremonies evident. But to which of the folks over on 14th Avenue, such as Thomas, did the law ever say "You shall become king ?" None. So there is basis now for recognizing Edward as king. But we are not to recognize Thomas as a co-regent, for there is no basis to so recognize him. It is not necessary to find an officially worded denial. Just the absence of an official affirmation is sufficient. We operate on the basis that Edward is king and Thomas is not. For this to be different, we would look for a change or amendment in the rules. Nor is it necessary that there be an officially written denial specifying that each of the other people in the land is not king. Just the absence of a positive, no official affirmation, in the present rules is adequate for us to recognize only Edward as king.

This is what Heb 1:5 is teaching with respect to Jesus and angels. There **is** in God's word an affirmation that Jesus is king. So we believe it, teach it and live by it. There is the absence of an affirmation in God's word that any angel is a

---

him that of the fruit of his body, according to the flesh, He would raise up the Christ to sit on his throne, [31] "he, foreseeing this, spoke concerning the resurrection of the Christ, that His soul was not left in Hades, nor did His flesh see corruption. [32] "This Jesus God has raised up, of which we are all witnesses. [33] "Therefore being exalted to the right hand of God, and having received from the Father the promise of the Holy Spirit, He poured out this which you now see and hear. [34] "For David did not ascend into the heavens, but he says himself: 'The LORD said to my Lord, Sit at My right hand, [35] Till I make Your enemies Your footstool." '[36] "Therefore let all the house of Israel know assuredly that God has made this Jesus, whom you crucified, both Lord and Christ."

king. So we do not believe it, teach it or live by it. The writer expects us to see that, due to the absence of an affirmation in God's word, we are to operate on the basis that no angel is king.

Another question to answer is, Is it also the case that there is no passage **denying** this of angels up to the time Hebrews was written? That is, is there silence during this time span, or just the absence of an affirmation?[113] The distinctions we are mentioning here are those between the generic Bible-unauthorized and its two specifics, silence and addressed prohibition. We dealt with this in Chapter 11. There, we were discussing actions. Heb 1:4-5 is discussing a truth.[114] It might prove helpful to express again the distinctions mentioned in Chapter 11.

When there is no affirmation, nothing on the positive side, nothing to which you can point letting you know the doctrine is okay, that doctrine is unauthorized. Further, since God is always consistent with Himself, then when the Bible prohibits something, this guarantees there is no affirmation of it (in the same covenant arrangement). So a Bible prohibition is a subset of the Bible unauthorized. Also,

---

[113] Mt 28:18-20 [18] "And Jesus came and spoke to them, saying, 'All authority has been given to Me in heaven and on earth. [19] 'Go therefore and make disciples of all the nations, baptizing them in the name of the Father and of the Son and of the Holy Spirit, [20] 'teaching them to observe all things that I have commanded you; and lo, I am with you always, *even* to the end of the age.' Amen." These words were expressed before Hebrews was written and deny that any angel is equal in authority with Christ. So this passage shows that the *no angel is king* doctrine in mind in Heb 1:5 is a Bible-addressed prohibition, and not a matter of Bible silence. However, as explained subsequently, since Heb 1:4-5 teaches that a Bible-unauthorized doctrine is forbidden, and all Bible-silent doctrines are unauthorized doctrines, then Heb 1:4-5 affirms Bible-silence forbids.

[114] But truth involves actions: the mental action of believing it, the action of teaching it and living according to that doctrine.

when there is Bible silence, there is no affirmation and no Bible-addressed prohibition. So when there is silence, there is no affirmation. Therefore, Bible silence also is a subset of the Bible-unauthorized. These relationships are depicted below. *All Bible-silence is Bible-unauthorized, but not all Bible-unauthorized is Bible silence. And all Bible-addressed prohibition is Bible-unauthorized, but not all Bible-unauthorized is Bible-addressed prohibition.*

The passage in Hebrews that we are studying speaks of Christ as king based on what God's word **did** say about Him. But the passage does not deny kingship to angels based on this. Rather, it does so based on what God's word **did not** say about them, a lack of affirmation. This is the unauthorized area. The passage is focusing our attention one step above Bible silence and Bible-addressed prohibition. It is focusing on the Bible-unauthorized generic, telling us **this** forbids belief in a doctrine.

Now, since when there is silence there is the absence of an affirmation, and since Heb 1:5 teaches that the absence of an affirmation forbids a doctrine, then Heb 1:5 is affirming Bible silence forbids.

Lastly, notice the time span covered by Heb 1:5: Backwards from the time the passage was written. This envelopes the times covered by the OT Scriptures from Genesis on, as well as NT times, all of what God had said up to the time Hebrews was written. So, for those addressed, *a Bible-unauthorized teaching is a forbidden teaching* was true during the whole time span covered in the OT as well into NT times. So, for those addressed, *a Bible-silent teaching is a forbidden teaching* also was true during the times covered in the OT as well as NT times.

Heb 1:13

Later, in the same chapter, are these words:

[13] But to which of the angels has He ever said: "Sit at My right hand, Till I make Your enemies Your footstool"?

This quotes from Ps 110:

[1]The LORD said to my Lord, "Sit at My right hand, Till I make Your enemies Your footstool." [2]The LORD shall send the rod of Your strength out of Zion. Rule in the midst of Your enemies! (Ps 110:1-2)

Again we see the superiority of Christ because God's word nowhere attributes to an angel what Ps 110 attributes to Christ: being ruler. All that we said about Heb 1:5 applies here.

116

Heb 5:1-10

This passage reads:

¹For every high priest taken from among men is appointed for men in things *pertaining* to God, that he may offer both gifts and sacrifices for sins. ² He can have compassion on those who are ignorant and going astray, since he himself is also subject to weakness. ³ Because of this he is required as for the people, so also for himself, to offer *sacrifices* for sins. ⁴ And no man takes this honor to himself, but he who is called by God, just as Aaron *was*.

⁵ So also Christ did not glorify Himself to become High Priest, *but it* was He who said to Him:

"You are My Son,
Today I have begotten You."

⁶ As *He* also *says* in another *place:*

"You *are* a priest forever
According to the order of Melchizedek";

⁷ who, in the days of His flesh, when He had offered up prayers and supplications, with vehement cries and tears to Him who was able to save Him from death, and was heard because of His godly fear, ⁸ though He was a Son, *yet* He learned obedience by the things which He suffered. ⁹ And having been perfected, He became the author of eternal salvation to all who obey Him, ¹⁰ called by God as High Priest "according to the order of Melchizedek."

Heb 5:5 quotes from Ps 2:7, reminding us of Heb 1:5. Heb 5:6 quotes from Ps 110:4, reminding us of Heb 1:13 (which quoted from Ps 110:1). Heb 5:10 repeats the affirmation in God's word that Christ is a high priest after the order of Melchizedek. Admittedly, Heb 5 does not raise a question like "To which angel or human being has God ever said, You are the antitype of the Melchizedek priesthood?" But this is not necessary, for we have already learned on two occasions in Hebrews the conclusion to draw when there is an absence of affirmation. Following Heb 1:5 and 1:13, we do not believe there is another antitype of the Melchizedek priesthood than Christ. For, in God's word, there is no such affirmation to be found.

Heb 7:20-22

We continue in Hebrews and notice 7:20-22:

[20] And inasmuch as *He was* not *made priest* without an oath [21] (for they have become priests without an oath, but He with an oath by Him who said to Him:

"The LORD has sworn
And will not relent,
'You *are* a priest forever
According to the order of Melchizedek' "),

[22] by so much more Jesus has become a surety of a better covenant.

This passage calls our attention to the institution of Christ's priesthood versus that of the Levitical priesthood. When Christ was made priest it was with a divine oath, according to the words of Ps 110 (Heb 7:21). But the Levitical priesthood was instituted **without** an oath. Here again we have a conclusion drawn as to the superiority of Christ (and his covenant). This is based on the absence in God's word of a positive teaching about the matter. Indeed, in Ex 27:21, where the institution of the Levitical priesthood is recorded, there is no divine oath. The passage reads:

> [21] "In the tabernacle of meeting, outside the veil which *is* before the Testimony, Aaron and his sons shall tend it from evening until morning before the LORD. *It shall be* a statute forever to their generations on behalf of the children of Israel.

And again, whether there is a passage somewhere in the Scriptures that **negatively** addresses the matter, a passage to which we can point that **actually denies** there was such an oath, is not deemed necessary to make the point. The absence of any positive statement teaching that there is such an oath is adequate.

Heb 7:13-14 with 8:4-5

But the word "nothing" is not used in Heb 1:5, 13; 5:1-10 or 7:20-21. It is in Heb 7:14. Let us now focus more on matters relating to chapter 7, and then on verse 14. Christ is described as a priest according to the order of Melchizedek, rather than according to the order of Aaron. This is to show that Christ is a better high priest than the OT high priests. The argument begins in chapter 5 (verses 6 and 10), continues in chapter 6 (verse 20), and now is the subject of chapter 7. Melchizedek typifies Christ and even the silence in Scripture about his father, mother, genealogy, beginning of days and end of days has significance (7:3, 16-17, 23-24). The silence in Scripture about Melchizedek's beginning and end pre-figures the continual nature of Christ's priesthood. This is in contrast with the repetition needed in the Aaronic lineage due to the death of those priests. Again, Christ is superior.

But the silence regarding Melchizedek (silence about his father, mother, genealogy, beginning of days and end of days in God's word) is typological silence. The silence that is the subject of Hebrews 7:14 is different. Notice the combination of Heb 7:13-14 and 8:4-5. Here we have Bible silence (the absence of an affirmation and the absence of a denial). Here we have Bible silence itself forbidding. The first passage reads:

> [13] For He of whom these things are spoken belongs to another tribe, from which no man has officiated at the altar. [14] For *it is* evident that our Lord arose from Judah, of which tribe Moses spoke nothing concerning priesthood.

Dods makes these observations about 7:14. He says the

> "to" (*eis*) in the verse is applied to the direction of the thought, as Acts 2.25 [David says to Him, GFB], aiming at Him. ... Compare our expression, "He spoke *to* such and such points." ... Whatever Moses spoke regarding priests was spoken with reference to another tribe and not with reference to Judah.[115]

A word-for-word rendering of the last half of Heb 7:14 reads, "to which tribe concerning priests nothing Moses spoke."

[115] Marcus Dods, *The Epistle to the Hebrews,* The Expositor's Greek Testament, ed. W. Robertson Nicoll (Grand Rapids: Wm. B. Eerdmans Publishing Company, 1970), IV, 312.

Nothing? What about the action concerning which the Bible teaches nothing? Can we engage in it with God's approval or not? Since Christ came from the tribe of Judah, and the referenced words of Moses said nothing about priests coming from this tribe, does this forbid? Was this adequate for concluding that, according to the law, Christ would not be a priest? Notice how the Spirit in Heb 8:4-5 answers:

> [4] For if He were on earth, He would not be a priest, since there are priests who offer the gifts according to the law; [5] who serve the copy and shadow of the heavenly things, as Moses was divinely instructed when he was about to make the tabernacle. For He said, "See *that* you make all things according to the pattern shown you on the mountain."

The Levitical priests left no room for a non-Levite like Jesus to serve as a priest. The last sentence in verse 5 is a quotation from Ex 25:40. Before and after this, God gives instruction to Moses about the tabernacle. Earlier, at Ex 25:9, God speaks of following the pattern "just so." And after verse 40, God continues to give instructions about the tabernacle. If we were to continue reading, we would find that instructions which instituted the Aaronic priesthood are provided in Ex 27:21-28:4. But here, nothing, not one thing, is said about priests coming from Judah – not a positive and not a negative (the "to specify is to exclude" claim notwithstanding).

So sons of Aaron, during OT times, could function as priests **according to the Law**, but not sons of Judah. Christ would not function as such a priest, therefore. So explains the Spirit in Heb 8:4-5. So Bible silence forbids was to be honored in OT times.

121

Heb 13:10-11

This passage reads:

[10] We have an altar from which those who serve the tabernacle have no right to eat. [11] For the bodies of those animals, whose blood is brought into the sanctuary by the high priest for sin, are burned outside the camp.

F.F. Bruce helps by explaining the OT background:

The sacrifice of Christ was the antitype of the sacrifice offered on the great day of atonement, and the flesh of the animals slaughtered in the course of that ritual was not eaten; their bodies were "carried forth without the camp" and there completely burned (Lev 16:27).[116] There were other sin-offerings in which this was not done; when the blood was not presented to God in the holy of holies, the flesh was eaten by the priests in the sanctuary. But since the blood of the bullock which made atonement for Aaron and his family, and of the goat which made atonement for the people, was carried into the holy of holies on the day of atonement, their bodies were incinerated. In other words, "they ... that serve the tabernacle" have no permission to eat from the altar which typically foreshadows the sacrifice of Christ. But the sacrifice of Christ is a better sacrifice,

---

[116] Lev 16:27 "The bull *for* the sin offering and the goat *for* the sin offering, whose blood was brought in to make atonement in the Holy *Place,* shall be carried outside the camp. And they shall burn in the fire their skins, their flesh, and their offal." (*Offal* means the undesirable or worthless parts of the burned animal, like the hooves and tail.) Commenting on Lev 16:27, Bruce adds a footnote: "So also with the sin-offerings of Ex 29:14; Lev 4:12; 8:17; 9:11."

not only because the spiritual antitype is superior to the
material type, but also because those who enter the
heavenly sanctuary "by the blood of Jesus" (Ch. 10:19)
know that the One who became their perfect sin-
offering is permanently available as the source of
spiritual nourishment ....[117]

In keeping with the repetitive argument in Hebrews, Heb
13:10-11 is a contrast between the OT and the better NT.
Several points of comparison are in mind:

- **We** *versus* **those.** We Christians. Those Israelites of the Levitical
  lineage who serve the tabernacle or temple.
- **OT altar** *versus* **NT altar.** The OT altar is the literal altar in the
  tabernacle and temple on which the animals referenced in Lev 16:27,
  for example, were sacrificed. The NT altar is the figurative "altar" on
  which Christ was sacrificed. This refers to what happened at the
  crucifixion (Heb 13:12).
- **OT eating of the sacrifice** *versus* **NT eating of the sacrifice.** The OT
  sacrifices in mind, as Bruce points out, are those animals that Lev
  16:27 and other OT passages forbade be eaten. The comparison
  showing that the NT is better turns on this. Christ is the antitypical
  fulfillment of these sacrifices and may be "eaten." Faithful Christians
  may "eat" Christ in the sense that they have continual access to the
  multiple blessings available in Him (Eph 1:3, 7).[118] One is reminded
  of the food metaphors in Jn 6:22-40. Another thought that comes to
  mind is the persecution in Mt 10:16-39: Christians should be willing
  to go "outside the gate," so to speak, to their Sacrifice.

---

[117] F. F. Bruce, *The Epistle to the Hebrews,* ed. F. F. Bruce, The New
International Commentary on the New Testament (Grand Rapids:Wm.
B. Eerdmans Publishing Co., 1964), 399.
[118] Eph 1:3, 7-8 ³Blessed *be* the God and Father of our Lord Jesus Christ, who
has blessed us with every spiritual blessing in the heavenly *places* in Christ,
... ⁷ In Him we have redemption through His blood, the forgiveness of sins,
according to the riches of His grace ⁸ which He made to abound toward us in
all wisdom and prudence.

123

Now let us notice this. The expression "have no right" in Heb 13:**10** translates the Greek *ouk echousin exousian*,[119] "they do not have authority." Heb 13:**11** is referring to an OT teaching taught, for example, in Lev 16:27. This passage in Leviticus implicitly forbade the Levitical priests to eat the sacrifice. (It is implicit and not explicit as seen by the fact that the sacrifice was to be taken outside the camp and burned up. Doing this **implies** they were not to eat it.) So verse 11 is pointing out that such an action is a Bible-addressed prohibition.

"For" in verse 11 is *gar* in the original Greek. This introduces verse 11 as the explanation for saying what is said in verse 10. This is so, although some claim that "for" here (*gar*) is not used in its regular sense of introducing an explanation or reason. Rather, they claim it is starting off verse 11 with an additive idea: "moreover," "in addition," or the like. Not taking "for" in its regular explanatory sense here apparently is due to their not seeing how verse 11 can possibly be an explanation of verse 10. But it is. Here is how: By referring to the Lev 16:27 prohibition in verse 11, the Spirit brings up the subject of an unauthorized action. (If an action is a prohibition, it is unauthorized.) Unauthorized is the generic that is one level above the prohibition of Lev 16:27. The specific in verse 11 gets us to the generic at the end of verse 10: They "have no right," "have no authority." Unlike those Israelites who had no authority to eat that sacrifice, Christians do have authority to "eat" their nearer Sacrifice. Thus, the overall point being made in verses 10-11 is that the NT is better than the OT.

---

[119] The dictionary form of this word, translated often as *power* or *authority,* is *exousia.* It "denotes the power which decides. ... [N]othing takes place apart from His [*exousia*] or authority." Werner Foerster, "εξουσια," *Theological Dictionary of the New Testament,* ed. Gerhand Kittel, trans. Geoffrey W. Bromiley (Grand Rapids: Wm. B. Eerdmans Publishing Company, 1964), II, 566. When Jesus was asked in the temple "By what authority (*exousia*) are You doing these things?", He spoke of two sources, "From heaven or from men." (Mt 21:23-27). He rejects the *from men* source (Mk 7:6-9). All legitimate authority is delegated authority by God. Within the guidelines of this, there is the freedom to act, and there can be wide latitude here.

En route, He focuses our attention on the problem of the **absence of authority FOR an action.** We already have learned from earlier passages in Hebrews that the unauthorized is forbidden. So, by focusing on the "unauthorized" generic, Heb 13:10 is like Heb 1:5; 1:13; 5:1-10 and 7:20-22. And, it is unlike the more specific Bible-silence forbids of Heb 7:13-14 with 8:4. It is also unlike the more specific Bible-addressed prohibition of Lev 16:27 referenced in Heb 13:11. All of this is illustrated below.

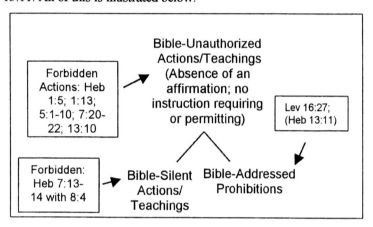

Further, since Heb 13:10-11, with earlier passages in Hebrews, teaches that the unauthorized is forbidden in OT times, and since all Bible-silent actions are Bible-unauthorized actions, then Heb 13:10-11 in its Hebrews context affirms Bible-silence forbids was true in OT times.

Now let us examine some objections to what we have studied in Chapter 17.

Objection

Regarding Heb 1:5; 1:13; 5:1-10; 7:20-22 and 13:10-11: You are saying that the absence in Scripture of any positive passage on an action is adequate for us to know we are not to teach or practice that action. This view cannot be reconciled with other uses of the OT in the NT:

(1) 2 Tim 3:8 says "Jannes and Jambres resisted Moses," yet these individuals are not mentioned in the OT.

(2) Speaking of what Moses thought, Acts 7:25 reads,

> "For he supposed that his brethren would have understood that God would deliver them by his hand, but they did not understand."

Yet, this is nowhere to be found in the OT Scriptures.

And,

(3) Jude 14-15 reads,

> [14] Now Enoch, the seventh from Adam, prophesied about these men also, saying, "Behold, the Lord comes with ten thousands of His saints, [15] "to execute judgment on all, to convict all who are ungodly among them of all their ungodly deeds which they have committed in an ungodly way, and of all the harsh things which ungodly sinners have spoken against Him."

Yet, where is such an attribution made to Enoch anywhere in the OT Scriptures? Nowhere.

Reply

The key is "adequate for **us** to know." Of course, as Heb 1:1 points out, God's word revealed additional information over time. If God in the NT, through an inspired writer, provides us with more information about anything, including an OT event, we can believe it and teach it. But we uninspired humans are not to go onward, beyond what God teaches. Heb 1:5, 13 and 7:20-22 show that we must stop our teaching just where God stopped. Do not go beyond this.

Objection

Heb 7:14 says that of Judah, Moses spoke nothing concerning priests. But of Judah and all the other non-Levitical tribes, Moses did speak something concerning priests. He does so in Num 16:36-40:

> [36] Then the LORD spoke to Moses, saying: [37] "Tell Eleazar, the son of Aaron the priest, to pick up the censers out of the blaze, for they are holy, and scatter the fire some distance away. [38] "The censers of these men who sinned against their own souls, let them be made into hammered plates as a covering for the altar. Because they presented them before the LORD, therefore they are holy; and they shall be a sign to the children of Israel." [39] So Eleazar the priest took the bronze censers, which those who were burned up had presented, and they were hammered out as a covering on the altar, [40] *to be* a memorial to the children of Israel that no outsider, who *is* not a descendant of Aaron, should come near to offer incense before the LORD, that he might not become like Korah and his companions, just as the LORD had said to him through Moses.

Notice "no outsider, who is not a descendant of Aaron, should come near to offer incense, ..." in verse 40. This covers the tribe of Judah. Something is wrong with what you are saying, therefore.

Reply

Let me summarize the reply in just a few words here in this paragraph, and then elaborate in the paragraphs that follow. Heb 7:14 is qualified, not unqualified. That is, the nothing in Heb 7:14 does not mean Moses said nothing **ever** about priests from Judah, as proved by Num 16:40. So given that Hebrews is the Word of God, the only possibility left is that **for a while**, Moses spoke nothing about priests coming from the tribe of Judah. There was a time when the words that Moses **did** speak about priests had nothing to say at all, negative or positive, about priests coming from Judah. Later, as seen in Num 16:40, Moses **did** add a prohibition forbidding all, except male Aaronic Levites. What Mosaic legislation on priesthood had nothing to say at all about priests from Judah? That which instituted the Levitical-Aaronic priesthood in Ex 27:21-28:4:

> [27:21] "In the tabernacle of meeting, outside the veil which *is* before the Testimony, Aaron and his sons shall tend it from evening until morning before the LORD. *It shall be* a statute forever to their generations on behalf of the children of Israel. [28:1] "Now take Aaron your brother, and his sons with him, from among the children of Israel, that he may minister to Me as priest, Aaron *and* Aaron's sons: Nadab, Abihu, Eleazar, and Ithamar. [2] "And you shall make holy garments for Aaron your brother, for glory and for beauty. [3] "So you shall speak to all *who are* gifted artisans, whom I have filled with the spirit of wisdom, that they may make Aaron's garments, to consecrate him, that he may minister to Me as priest. [4] "And these *are* the garments which they shall make: a breastplate, an ephod, a robe, a skillfully woven tunic, a turban, and a sash. So they shall make holy garments for Aaron your brother and his sons, that he may minister to Me as priest.

Unlike Num 16:40, there is nothing in this passage about priests from Judah.[120]

Now let me elaborate. At first glance, it might appear that Heb 7:14 means "of Judah Moses spoke nothing at all ever about priests." But when we look at the whole council of God, the wider Biblical context, we see that Heb 7:14 is not so unqualified in meaning. Num 16:40 shows this. There, Moses did say something of Judah about priests, namely an implicit prohibition. It is hard to believe, even from a human standpoint, that the Hebrews writer, whose book so often refers to the OT Scriptures and to the priesthood, was unaware of this passage in Numbers. And surely, the Holy Spirit did not forget what He said in Numbers. The wider Biblical context shows that Heb 7:14 is more limited in scope than one might at first think.

This happens in Scripture. As another example, one could read Roman 10:9-10. From this one might conclude that belief and confession of belief are all that are necessary to become saved. There is not a word in the passage about repentance or baptism - nothing. Yet, from other Biblical passages (Acts 2:38; ...), we see that these conditions are added, thus giving us the fuller picture. Or, one reads about Christ's divorce law in Lk 16:18. But "except for fornication" is not to be found either in this passage, or in its immediate context, or even in the more remote context in the whole book of Luke. But when we read another Bible book, and two chapters in that book (Mt 5, Mt 19), we find the exception and thus see the fuller picture. And was "This is the King of the Jews" all that was written on the

---

[120] What would we say to those who deny that the Bible is the Word of God and who might use Heb 7:14 and Num 16:40 to show a conflict? All we need is the possibility of reconciling the two passages to show that such deniers have no clincher here.

cross? Some might answer Yes from Lk 19:38. But Jn 19:19 shows there was more. Scripture can qualify Scripture. We need to see the fuller picture before we conclude.

The moment you find **something** that Moses said about having priests from Judah (like the prohibition in Num 16:40, "… no outsider, who *is* not a descendant of Aaron, …"), you have then found that to which Heb 7:14 is not referring. The "nothing" in Heb 7:14 means "not one thing." The passage is saying, of the tribe of Judah, Moses spoke not one thing concerning priesthood. Notice this: (1) An explicit prohibition is one thing. (2) An implied prohibition is one thing. (3) An explicit requirement is one thing. (4) An implicit requirement is one thing. (5) An explicit option is one thing. (6) An implicit option is one thing. Only when legislation has none of these regarding a matter does that legislation legislate **not** one thing about that matter. And the passage teaches that, of the tribe of Judah, it is the case that Moses said **not** one thing about priesthood. So of Judah, Moses said none of these six something's concerning priesthood. Yet, in Num 16:40, of Judah Moses does say something (one thing) concerning priesthood. He provides an implied prohibition (our number 2 above).

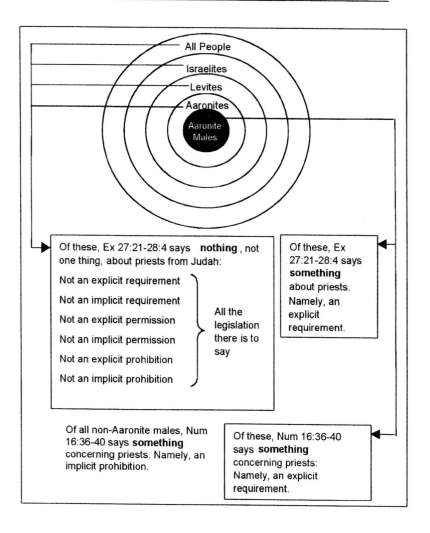

All People

Israelites

Levites

Aaronites

Aaronite Males

Of these, Ex 27:21-28:4 says **nothing**, not one thing, about priests from Judah:

Not an explicit requirement

Not an implicit requirement

Not an explicit permission

Not an implicit permission

Not an explicit prohibition

Not an implicit prohibition

All the legislation there is to say

Of these, Ex 27:21-28:4 says **something** about priests. Namely, an explicit requirement.

Of all non-Aaronite males, Num 16:36-40 says **something** concerning priests. Namely, an implicit prohibition.

Of these, Num 16:36-40 says **something** concerning priests: Namely, an explicit requirement.

131

Now, there has to be enough space in what Moses said about the Levitical-Aaronic priesthood which allows for the nothing in Heb 7:14, or there is a conflict. So where is this space? What is the reference? Look before Num 16. Look at the **institution** of the Levitical priesthood, not to the later information eventually added to this. The "nothing" in Heb 7:14 is not nothing ever (Num 16:40), but nothing when the priesthood was instituted (Ex 27:21-28:1). The revelation of God was progressive. Information on a topic may be revealed, and then more and more added later. This is what we have with the Levitical priesthood. At first, Aaron and his sons are mentioned as the lineage from which priests were to be taken. But nothing, pro **or con**, is said about the non Levitical-Aaronic people functioning as priests. Notice this absence in the last verse of Ex 27 (verse 21), and the first verse of Ex 28, where we read of the institution, the inauguration, of the Levitical priesthood:

27:21 "In the tabernacle of meeting, outside the veil which *is* before the Testimony, Aaron and his sons shall tend it from evening until morning before the LORD. *It shall be* a statute forever to their generations on behalf of the children of Israel.

28:21 "Now take Aaron your brother, and his sons with him, from among the children of Israel, that he may minister to Me as priest, Aaron *and* Aaron's sons: Nadab, Abihu, Eleazar, and Ithamar.

Eventually, in Ex 28:12, all 12 tribes are referenced. But this pertains to the ephod Aaron was to wear. There is nothing here about any tribe outside of Aaron's lineage functioning as priests, the subject of Heb 7:14. The children of Israel are again mentioned in verses 21, 29 and 38. But still nothing on our subject. It is not until we get to Ex 29:32-34 that we learn of a **prohibition** that seems relevant to our subject:

> [32] "Then Aaron and his sons shall eat the flesh of the ram, and the bread that *is* in the basket, *by* the door of the tabernacle of meeting. [33] "They shall eat those things with which the atonement was made, to consecrate *and* to sanctify them; but an outsider shall not eat *them,* because they *are* holy. [34] "And if any of the flesh of the consecration offerings, or of the bread, remains until the morning, then you shall burn the remainder with fire. It shall not be eaten, because it *is* holy.

But even here one wonders how wide a prohibition this is, without the benefit of clearer passages later given. More along these lines is given subsequently, for example in Num 3:10:

> So you shall appoint Aaron and his sons, and they shall attend to their priesthood; but the outsider who comes near shall be put to death.

However, it is hard to claim any mystery about who is included in "the outsider" in Num 16:36-40. So the information telling of who would be priests starts off by specifying Aaron and his sons from the tribe of Levi, with nothing said about the other tribes. Not until later do we have information that actually forbids all the other tribes, thus forbidding Judah. (See also 1 Sam 6:19[121]; 2 Sam 6:6-11[122] ; 2 Chron 26:18.[123])

Now, there is a different conclusion to consider. Ex 27:21-28:1 by itself **is** adequate and remained so for the Israelites to have known that *priests are to come only from Levi until and if God allows them to come from any non-Levitical tribe.* The matter can be summed up by posing two questions to an Israelite living during the time the former covenant was being revealed:

1. Is it God's will in this Covenant that you only have priests from Levi?
2. Will it be God's will during this Covenant that you only have priests from Levi?

---

[121] 1 Sam 6:19 "Then He struck the men of Beth Shemesh, because they had looked into the ark of the Lord. He struck fifty thousand and seventy men of the people, and the people lamented because the Lord had struck the people with a great slaughter. "

[122] 2 Sam 6:6-11 "And when they came to Nachon's threshing floor, Uzzah put out *his hand* to the ark of God and took hold of it, for the oxen stumbled [7]then the anger of the Lord was aroused against Uzzah, and God struck him there for *his* error; and he died there by the ark of God. [8]And David became angry because of the Lord's outbreak against Uzzah; and he called the name of the place Perez Uzzah to this day. [9]David was afraid of the Lord that day; and he said, 'How can the ark of the Lord come to me?' [10]So David would not move the ark of the Lord with him into the City of David; but David took it aside into the house of Obed-Edom the Gittite. [11]The ark of the Lord remained in the house of Obed-Edom the Gittite three months. And the Lord blessed Obed-Edom and all his household."

[123] 2 Chron 26:18 "And they withstood King Uzziah, and said to him, '*It is* not for you, Uzziah, to burn incense to the Lord, but for the priests, the sons of Aaron, who are consecrated to burn incense. Get out of the sanctuary, for you have trespassed! You *shall have* no honor from the Lord God.'"

134

Answering **only** with the revelation up to and including Ex 27:21-28:1:

1. Yes. (Remember now that the Hebrews writer has shown us that *unauthorized* forbids - *the absence of an affirmation* forbids - was true throughout the times covered by the OT scriptures.)
2. I cannot tell.

Answering with the revelation that includes Ex 27:21-28:1 and Num 16:40 **combined**:

1. Yes.
2. Yes.

If we claim Yes to both questions with only the Ex 27:21-28:1 information, we are in conflict with Heb 7:14. This is so because we would be claiming this OT passage teaches something about priests from Judah while Hebrews 7:14 says it teaches nothing about it. Notice that the "to specify is to exclude" claim leaves no space even in Ex 27:21-28:1 for the nothing of Heb 7:14. That "law" of exclusion claims that the moment Moses specified Aaron and his sons, he thereby excludes all the other tribes. That law of exclusion thus leaves no space even here for the nothing of Heb 7:14. But Ex 27:21-28:1, which institutes the Levitical priesthood, does leave space for the nothing. So the objection we have been reviewing fails. A brief commentary on Heb 7:14 could read, "not nothing ever (Num 16:36-40), but nothing when the Aaronic-Levitical priesthood was instituted (Ex 27:21-28:4)."

Chapter 18
Bible Silence Permits
Claims (1)

Several assertions and arguments have been advanced to deny Bible silence forbids (BSF) and/or to affirm Bible silence permits (BSP). Chapters 18 through 20 identify and critique some of these claims. In this chapter we will examine the following:

- Rom 4:15 proves BSP
- The silence of the Bible is insignificant
- BSF binds human doctrine
- BSF is mere borrowed tradition
- BSF would forbid congregational singing

Rom 4:15 Proves BSP
Some claim that the last half of Rom 4:15 shows that Bible silence permits. The passage reads:

> because the law brings about wrath; for where there is no law *there is* no transgression.

They call our attention to "for where there is no law there is no transgression." They are saying "no law" can be replaced with "silence," resulting in the meaning "where there is silence, there is no transgression." That is, they take the passage to mean, "when God is silent on an action, we may or may not do the action and be right with Him either way."

For the silence permits defender to prove his case from this passage, it would have to be the case that either "silence" and "no law" are equivalent, or at least that silence is an instance of no law. So, if it can be shown that, when there is Bible silence on an action, there still exists law on that action, then it will have been shown that the passage does not prove silence permits. Let's show this, and then focus on what the passage does mean.

First, for there to be **no** law from God when the Bible is silent on an action it would have to be that the Bible is silent on how to interpret its silence. Otherwise, there would be a law in existence and thus not *no law*. But it is false that the Bible is silent on its silence. As we have shown in previous chapters, 2 Tim 3:16-17 with 1 Thes 5:21 (or Col 3:17, ...) may be used successfully to show that there **is** law from God concerning silence. It is not the case, then, that when the Bible is silent on an action there is no law on that action. So *silence* and *no law* are not equivalent, and silence is not an instance of no law. Therefore, the silence permits defender who cites this passage to support the doctrine is misusing the passage.

Second, there is another line of reasoning which shows that when there is Bible silence there is law. The very claim the silence permits defender is making about the verse is self-contradictory and therefore false. Notice this carefully. He is claiming Rom 4:15 teaches silence permits in that silence is "no law." But if we have God's permission regarding an action, we

do have law from God on that action. His law would be that we have his permission. We can see this even regarding government matters. When the government tells us we have permission to build a house on Lot A, this is existing law regarding that matter. The same principle is true regarding the Master. When, for example, we know the Lord has forbidden an action, we know that his law is that the action is forbidden. When we know that he requires an action, we know that his law is that the action is required. When we know he permits an action, we know that his law is that the action is permitted (optional). It is not the case that law only includes a must-not-do or a must-do. **Permission** is an instance of law, **not** an instance of **no** law (**not** the absence of law). So the interpretation of Rom 4:15 which we are examining forces one into silliness (contradiction). It forces him into saying there is **no law** while claiming there is law from God (the alleged permission – Bible silence permits). This contradiction shows that the silence permits defender who cites the passage as proof for his position is misinterpreting the passage: God's word does not contradict itself.

Third, in fact the silence permits defender is taking the passage to mean **exactly** the opposite of its intended meaning. To prove his case from this passage, he is claiming that the statement "where there is no law there is no transgression" affirms that the first part of this statement ("there is no law") is true. But the Holy Spirit wants us to see that the statement "there is no law" is false. Rom 5 tells us that sin results in death (verse 12) and death reigned since Adam's time. So there has been God's law since Adam. By "Where there is no law there is no transgression" in Rom 4, the Holy Spirit does not mean there **are** human actions concerning which God has made no law. Rather, the Spirit's message is that all accountable people **have** sinned, and therefore each of us has violated some **existing** law of God. Further, we are to see that this is what sin

138

is: The violation of God's law. The Spirit expects us to see that since the second part of the statement ("there is no transgression") is false, then the first part ("there is no law") also is **false**[124] (not **true,** as the silence permits defender who cites this verse is claiming). There **is** sin is the Spirit's point. There **are** sinners. And we are they. The Spirit is telling us that we are sinners and therefore need to follow Jesus Christ so that we can be forgiven of these sins. This is his message.

He expresses the **false** statement "there is no transgression" here in Rom 4:15 (and expects us to see that it is false). He deals with the opposite side, the **true** statement, on two occasions in the preceding chapter:

> [9] What then? Are we better *than they?* Not at all. For we have previously charged both Jews and Greeks that they are all under sin. (Rom 3:10)

> [23] for all have sinned and fall short of the glory of God (Rom 3:23)

The knowledge that each of these statements in Chapter 3 is true tells us that the "there is no transgression" part of 4:15 is false. As we have already mentioned, knowing that the statement "there is no transgression" in 4:15 is false, leads us to see that the preceding statement in 4:15 ("there is no law") also must be false.

---

[124] A logical move called "denying the consequent." Also called *modus tollens.*

That this is the Spirit's meaning, rather than the silence permits interpretation (that "there is no law" is **true**) is confirmed by the information provided for us in the wider context: Rom 1 through 4. In case we might miss this, the Spirit has given us signals in and around 4:15 which tie us to the context. He does this by including words like "for" and "because" in verses 13, 14 and 15, and "therefore" which starts verse 16. "For" and "because" here translate the Greek word *gar* which introduces an explanation of previous information. "Therefore" (in the Greek here, *dia touto, "on account of this")* signals he is drawing a conclusion from the previous information. Notice these terms in the passage (emphasis is mine, GFB.):

> [13] **For** (*gar*) the promise that he would be the heir of the world *was* not to Abraham or to his seed through the law, but through the righteousness of faith. [14] **For** (*gar*) if those who are of the law *are* heirs, faith is made void and the promise made of no effect, [15] **because** (*gar*) the law brings about wrath; for where there is no law *there is* no transgression. [16] **Therefore** *(dia touto)* it is of faith that *it might be* according to grace, so that the promise might be sure to all the seed, not only to those who are of the law, but also to those who are of the faith of Abraham, who is the father of us all

In Rom 1 through 4, the Spirit has been explaining that **both** Jews and gentiles are sinners in need of God's grace to be saved. Every person who was, is or ever will be saved, is saved by faith (an obedient faith), not by meritorious works: No one saves himself by perfectly following all of God's laws, never sinning, thus having no need for God's grace.

140

Rather, every accountable Jew is a sinner. Every accountable gentile is a sinner. Since all of us, therefore, are in one of these two categories, then all of us are sinners. So all of us have violated **existing** laws of God, since this is what sin is: Rom 3:10 and Rom 3:23; compare 1 Jn 3:4.

He repeats this message in reverse in Rom 4:15, and expects us to see by now that the expression "there is no transgression" in this passage is **false** and therefore "there is no law" in the passage is **false**. But, if we cite Rom 4:15 to prove silence permits, we then take "there is no law" as true. (Remember, now, silence permits folks grant there are human actions about which the Bible is silent and that "there is no law" here is referring to such actions.) We would thus be taking as true what the Holy Spirit intends us to take as false. So then, we encourage the beloved silence permits defender no longer to teach people the opposite of the passage. But to join the Holy Spirit in God's truth: There is no law is **false**, not **true!**

The Silence of the Bible Is Insignificant

Some claim that Bible silence is insignificant or unintentional and therefore we should not base much on it. For example, Randy Fenter has articulated this thinking. He did so in a paper he delivered in the Oklahoma Christian University Lectureship in 1989. The paper is titled "Do Not Go Beyond What Is Written." The essence of the paper was repeated in a three-part article by Fenter in the August, September and October, 1989 issues of *Image Magazine*. We will let Fenter express the doctrine for us. Under the heading "Is the New Testament a Constitution" in the September issue of *Image*, he writes:

141

Is the New Testament a constitution of church law, or is it a collection of epistles?[125]

If the form of the New Testament is constitutional, then silence is intentional and necessarily prohibitive of anything not explicitly found in Scripture.[126]

On the other hand, if Scripture is a collection of God-given, Holy Spirit-inspired letters addressed to real people with real needs, then silence is not inherently prohibitive. Silence simply means that the particular issue under discussion was not addressed in those God-given letters.[127]

Fenter then quotes Mike Armour from a class "at the 1988 Abilene Christian Lectureship." Armour offers the illustration of two kinds of documents:

- a collection of letters he wrote to his wife during their courtship, and
- the bylaws of Columbia Christian College which he drafted when he was President there.

Then, Fenter continues, Armour explained that the bylaws document anticipates every eventuality, so its silence is intentional. But the letters are different. Their "silence is insignificant. Just because I don't write to my fiance about certain topics doesn't give you any insight about what I think about those topics." Then the question is raised, Is the Bible a constitution like the bylaws or, rather, is it like these love letters

---

[125] Fenter, p. 9. See footnote 84 for bibliographical information.

[126] Fenter, p. 9.

[127] Fenter, p. 9.

142

that were "dashed off by an apostle to a church that he has some specific concerns about"?

Fenter proceeds to quote Larry James for another "consideration:"

The New Testament was never intended to be a 'legal brief' for the church through the ages. We must not assign a purpose to the text of Scripture which the writers never intended."[128]

In other words, the answer to the question is that the Bible is like Armour's love letters and not like a constitution. So Bible silence is insignificant and thus not binding (by which some mean, in practice, Bible silence permits). What shall we say about this?

First, I have already shown how Fenter fails to see the difference between implication and silence in his "if, then" statement:

If the form of the New Testament is constitutional, then silence is intentional and necessarily prohibitive of anything not explicitly found in Scripture.

See "What Do You Mean by Silence?" in Chapter 10.

Second, the Bible cannot correctly be characterized as being one kind of document. It consists of biography, history, letters to individuals, letters to groups. But within these are commands, declarative statements, interrogatives, constituting requirements, prohibitions, and permissions. For example, we are taught the **requirement** of following God's word to be

---

[128] Fenter, p. 10.

saved by a **question** in Heb 2:1-4. Hebrews is a **letter** that closes with the expressed wish that God will make its readers complete in "every good work" (Heb 12:21). Then the text says, expressed as a **command**, "And I appeal to you, brethren, bear with the word of exhortation, ..." (Heb 12:22) We are taught the same **requirement** by means of a **command** in the **letter** from James in Jas 2:21-22:

> [21] ... receive with meekness the implanted word, which is able to save your souls. [22] But be doers of the word, and not hearers only, deceiving yourselves.

In a **biography** book, at Mk 16:15-16, we learn from a **declarative statement** that obeying God in baptism is a **requirement** for forgiveness. We learn the same truth by **command** in a **history** book at Acts 2:38. Its urgency is taught by a **question** at the beginning of Acts 22:16. We learn that this baptism is a requirement by a **declarative statement** in a **letter** at 1 Pet 3:20-21. Further, we learn that lying is a **prohibition** by means of a **command** in the **letter to a group** at Eph 4:28, by a **declarative statement** in a **letter to an individual** at 1 Tim 1:8-11, by a **declarative statement** in a **letter to a group** at Rev 21:8. We learn by a **declarative statement** in Rom 14:2-3 that being a vegetarian or not is an **option**. The same teaching is reiterated in a **question** in Rom 14:4. In all of this we see great wisdom maintaining our attention as readers and listeners. We see that God distributed his all-sufficient regulations throughout a variety of literary forms familiar in daily life. We see warmth, tenderness, care, discipline. Together, they provide a pattern, a blueprint, a constitution directing us toward righteous living so we can go to heaven.

Third, the Bible views the **whole** assemblage of its parts as being all sufficient for equipping its readers with **all good** works (2 Tim 3:16-17). So, if a work is good, it is in the Bible, taught as such either explicitly or implicitly. And if a work is not in there (that is, if there is nothing in the Bible which addresses that work, the Bible is silent on it), then that work is not a good work. Silence, therefore, in a book from **God** which claims to be **all sufficient**, is intended and meaningful silence, not insignificant silence. Bible silence is an intended means by which God conveys His will. Let us have confidence in it.

BSF Binds Human Doctrine

Some claim that Bible silence forbids imposes human doctrine on others, thus violating Mt 15:8-9. The passage reads:

> [8]'These people draw near to Me with their mouth, And honor Me with *their* lips, But their heart is far from Me. [9] And in vain they worship Me, Teaching *as* doctrines the commandments of men.'

For this passage to apply, it would have to be that the Bible silence forbids doctrine has its origin in men and not in God. But God's word itself teaches the doctrine in 2 Tim 3:16-17 with 1 Thes 5:21; Heb 7:13-14 with 8:4; and Col 3:17. So Mt 15:8-9 does not apply to the Bible silence forbids doctrine.

BSF Is Mere Borrowed Tradition

Some claim that Bible silence forbids is mere tradition borrowed from Calvinistic groups. *First*, tradition means a handing down of doctrine. Mere human doctrine replacing God's can be handed down. This is forbidden according to Mt 15:8-9. But God's doctrine, now in the Bible, also can be handed down. This is required according to 2 Thes 2:15:

> Therefore, brethren, stand fast and hold the traditions which you were taught, whether by word or our epistle.

Since we have shown that the Bible teaches its silence forbids, then by teaching this we are handing down God's doctrine in keeping with 2 Thes 2:15, and not handing down mere human doctrine in violation of Mt 15:8-9.

Second, the fact that a professed Christian group teaches false doctrine in one area does not prove they teach false doctrine in this area. Further, the fact that they teach Bible truth in an area, and did so before I was born, does not somehow show that I ought not to hand down the same truth. If the Bible teaches the doctrine, this is all I need, whether or not someone else may have taught the same doctrine who lived between the Bible and me. This is true, even if it were the case that I first learned this **Bible** truth from someone who teaches error in another area. Even this would not somehow change Bible tradition into mere human tradition. All that counts is whether or not the Bible teaches the doctrine. And, as we have shown, the Bible does teach that its silence forbids. So we ought to continue handing down the Bible silence forbids doctrine, regardless of who else may or may not have done so.

BSF Would Exclude Congregational Singing

Some claim that the Bible silence forbids doctrine, if consistently applied, would forbid congregational singing. Retired editor of the *Christian Standard,* Edwin V. Hayden, writes,

> Prohibition-by-silence would, in fact, rule out congregational singing in public meetings of the church. It is nowhere commanded, indicated, or exemplified in Holy Writ.[129]

He then takes up several NT passages on singing, denying they provide proof for congregational singing. For example, he says,

> Christians as individuals in the everyday home setting were exhorted to teach and encourage one another with songs of various kinds (Ephesians 5:19; Colossians 3:16), but nothing is said of singing praises to God together in church![130]

And,

> First Corinthians 14:15 and 26 do mention songs in the context of the public meeting. Paul said he would sing with the spirit and the understanding, but did not mention *group* singing.[131]

Hayden is mistaken. There **is** NT authority for congregational singing. Eph 5 is sufficient to show this.

---

[129] Edwin V. Hayden, "An Unbearable Yoke" (Cincinnati: *The Christian Standard,* June 23, 1985) p. 6.
[130] Hayden, p. 6.
[131] Hayden, p. 6.

Eph 5:15-21 reads,

> [15] See then that you walk circumspectly, not
> as fools but as wise, [16] redeeming the time,
> because the days are evil. [17] Therefore do not
> be unwise, but understand what the will of
> the Lord *is*. [18] And do not be drunk with
> wine, in which is dissipation; but be filled
> with the Spirit, [19] speaking to one another in
> psalms and hymns and spiritual songs,
> singing and making melody in your heart to
> the Lord, [20] giving thanks always for all
> things to God the Father in the name of our
> Lord Jesus Christ, [21] submitting to one
> another in the fear of God.

The following combination of facts from this passage
constitute sufficient evidence to imply authority for
congregational singing. *First,* "spiritual songs" combined with
"to the Lord" cover worship of God by singing.

Second, the actions mentioned are to be done by more than
one person. So this is a group of Christians singing in worship
of God. Note the plural subjects: "one another," "not as fools,"
the Greek plurals "you walk," the plural participles
"redeeming," "speaking," "singing," "giving thanks,"
"submitting." We notice that the passage does not specify a
certain plural number such as two, ten or whatever. Rather, it is
generic as to the plurality. So, it covers any plural number. If
there are two, it covers the two. If there are 2000, it covers the
2000. And, in this passage, all in the group are to do what is
indicated.

Third, here is an action these plural subjects are to do: "speaking to one another in psalms and hymns and spiritual songs, singing and making melody in your heart to the Lord." There is no limiting term indicated in the immediate or remote Biblical context, no qualifier, as to the physical place where the Christians are to do this. So the group of Christians who come together to do this action, whether they number 2 or 200, whether they meet in an auditorium, in the basement of a house, or in a field under the oak tree, singing "Standing on the promises of Christ my King" fits within the generic boundaries of the passage.

Fourth, Hayden's claim that this is "everyday home settings" is not in the passage. The passage has certain generics indicated, but this limiting specific Hayden mentions is not in there. And when God is generic on matters, we can be generic on those matters. Generic authority includes all specifics that implement it, except of course any elsewhere prohibited.

Fifth, notice Hayden's words *said* and *mention*:

- "but nothing is said of singing praises to God together in church!" and
- Paul "did not mention *group* singing."

He is insisting that we find "church" singing or "group" singing actually mentioned, or we are forced to say there is silence on such singing and, if we are consistent, that such action is therefore prohibited. This imposes the explicit-only error on us, and confuses silence with implication. The truth is that the words which **are** in the Bible cover (imply) group singing, as we have shown.

In conclusion, the passage specifies kinds of action and plurality. One of these actions is worshiping God in song. But the passage is generic as to "how plural," leaving the number unlimited. It is also generic as to where the specified actions are to be done. Congregational singing (group singing, church singing) is thus covered by the passage's meaning. So, the Bible is not silent on congregational singing. So it is incorrect to claim that the Bible silence forbids doctrine excludes congregational singing. The doctrine excludes from righteousness only those actions concerning which the Bible is silent.

Chapter 19
Bible Silence Permits Claims (2)

This chapter deals with the following claims:

- When God accepts the person, that person's acts of worship are permitted

- The naming of Jesus and John disproves BSF

- BSF would forbid modern things

- BSF would paralyze us into non-action

When God Accepts a Person, That Person's Acts of Worship Are Permitted

In his debate with Alan Highers, Given O. Blakely said,

> In the new covenant it is the *person* that is authorized, not merely the deed.[132]

---

[132] Given O. Blakely in *The Highers-Blakely Debate on Instrumental Music* (Denton, TX: Valid Publications, Inc., 1988) p. 66. This oral debate was conducted in Neosho, Missouri on April 12-15, 1988.

It is a diversionary tactic to turn our attention away to what we *do* – whether it is accepted. It is whether *we* are accepted that is the issue. Whether *you* have been received is the point. God has received *us* in Christ Jesus. Oh, that men would see it more. ... Now for an accepted person to worship unacceptably seems to me to be an incongruous and illogical thought.[133]

This is another way of saying that, regarding the Christian's worship of God, Bible silence permits.

First, from Blakely's words, it would be appropriate now to ask questions about four areas of human activity. (1) the Christian's worship activities., (2) the Christian's non-worship activities, (3) the non-Christian's worship activities and (4) the non-Christian's non-worship activities? With the words above, Blakely is referring to (1). What of the other three areas? The fact is that the inclusive language in 2 Tim 3:16-17, 1 Thes 5:21 and Col 3:17 applies the BSF doctrine to all human activity. (If one were to try to apply a silence doctrine only to some human actions, then he is left to explain (1) Which ?, (2) What is God's will regarding the other human activities about which He is silent ? and (3) What Scriptures do you cite to establish your answers to (1) and (2)?

---

[133] Blakely, p. 66.

Second, God's acceptance of a person is based on the person's meeting God's conditions for acceptance. This includes but is not limited to worship:

> God *is* Spirit, and those who worship Him must worship in spirit and truth. (Jn 4:24)

> But in every nation whoever fears Him and works righteousness is accepted by Him. (Acts 10:35)

> And do not be conformed to this world, but be transformed by the renewing of your mind, that you may prove what *is* that good and acceptable and perfect will of God. (Rom 12:2)

> ... to present you holy, and blameless, and above reproach in His sight— [23] if indeed you continue in the faith, grounded and steadfast, and are not moved away from the hope of the gospel which you heard .... (Col 1:22-23)

Third, as to worship activities, look carefully at Jn 4:24 again:

> God *is* Spirit, and those who worship Him must worship in spirit and truth.

The word "**must**" coupled with "**truth**" in this passage addresses the very point at hand. Jesus is teaching us here that we **do** need God's authority for our worship to be acceptable to him.

153

The Naming of Jesus
and John Disproves BSF

Edwin V. Hayden attempts to refute the Bible silence forbids doctrine with another claim. He writes,

> Prohibition-by-silence would have prevented the Lord's followers from calling Him *Master, Teacher, Lord,* or *Robboni.* The divine mandate was to call His name Jesus. Period! (Matthew 1.21; Luke 1:31). Similarly, prohibition-by-silence would have forbidden the addition of *Baptist* or *Immerser* to the name John. The angel Gabriel told Zacharias that the promised baby's name was to be John. Period! (Luke 1:13). Ridiculous application? Of course it is. But that is the direction of prohibition-by-silence.[134]

Here, Hayden is refuting a false law of exclusion which some silence forbids defenders use, and he thinks he has thereby refuted the silence forbids doctrine itself. We are dealing with two laws of exclusion here, and we need to distinguish them: (1) Bible silence excludes (forbids) and (2) A required specific excludes (forbids). He is refuting the second, and thinks he is refuting the first. But Bible silence forbids does not depend on the law of exclusion he is refuting. So what he says leaves the Bible silence forbids doctrine untouched. Let us talk more about the law of exclusion at which he is aiming, and then show it is not relevant to Bible silence forbids. (You may want to read

---

[134] Hayden, p. 5. One could study the meaning of "name" at this time (*onoma* in the Greek) to see if a distinction between name and title might be relevant. But notice that *onoma* can refer both to "Jesus" (Mt 1:21) and "Son" (Heb 1:4-5).

ahead by going to Chapter 22. That chapter concentrates on this second law of exclusion, showing it is false. There I examine in detail the explanation which J. D. Thomas asserts about this law in his book *We Be Brethren*, a book which otherwise contains helpful information. Here, in the present discussion, I critique this law of exclusion more briefly and show it is not relevant to Bible silence forbids.

The Wrong "Law" of Exclusion

This "law" of exclusion is worded different ways. Here are some of the ways you might hear it expressed:

- A required specific excludes.
- To specify is to exclude.
- Required specifics exclude from righteousness.
- A required specific excludes any or all additional actions on its level.

Toward a more complete way of saying it is "Required specifics exclude from righteousness (forbid) all other specifics which are under the same generic as that required specific." Still another way of saying it is "Requiring a specific action **implies** the denial of **all** other specific actions in the same class." (Note, however, that if by "to specify is to exclude" one means only "to require action x is to forbid all **substitutions** for action x," there is no objection to such a concept. See this exception discussed on page 212. But I advise being clearer: Saying "to specify is to exclude" to convey only this idea to your audience could result in your being misunderstood. You might be taken to mean that it is the specific that forbids **all** other specifics in the class, including accompanying specifics.)

The incorrect idea can be expressed in a diagram:

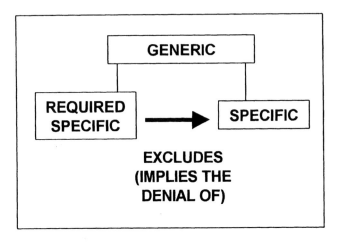

Applying this law, it is said that God's specifying to Noah that he build the ark out of gopher wood is what excluded any other kind of wood. Another example is God's requiring that fruit of the vine be used in the Lord's Supper is what excludes any other kind of liquid. (Actually, the silence, the lack of authority for, any other kind of wood and the silence of any other kind of liquid is what excludes these, because Bible silence forbids.)

If the *to specify is to exclude* idea were a true law, then the OT requirement to sing in Ps 68:32 (a required specific under the music generic), conflicted with (implied the denial of, did not leave room for) the OT requirement to use the instrument in Ps 150 (another specific under the same music generic). Since the Bible does not conflict with itself, then Ps 68:32 with Ps 150 is sufficient to show we are dealing with a false law of exclusion. This is illustrated below.

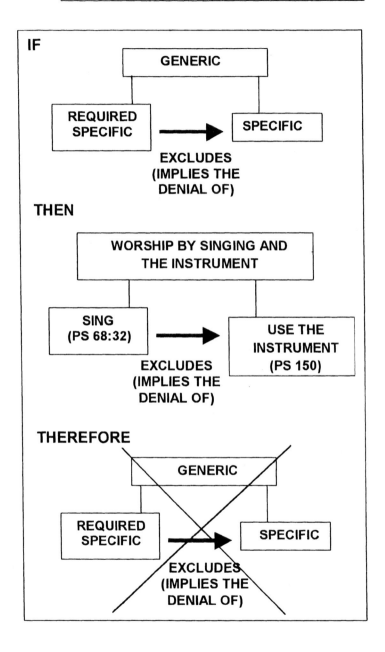

In his article, where he is refuting this "law", Hayden expresses the law like this: "... every affirmative command of God is also a negative ...."[135] That by this he means *the required specifics exclude* claim is clear from the refutation he offers: If this alleged law of God were true, he is reasoning, then it would follow that the Mt 1:21 requirement of calling Jesus Jesus would exclude all other names of Jesus. And it would also follow that the Lk 1:13 requirement of calling John John would exclude all other names of John. One could diagram what Hayden is getting at as follows.

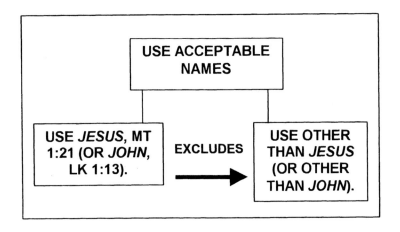

The act of calling Jesus with acceptable name(s) is the generic action. Mt 1:21 is the required specific under this generic. And the other Biblical references to Him are the other specifics under this same generic. (Note Son – Heb 1:4-5, Teacher and Christ – Mt 23:6-10, God and Savior – Titus 2:13, Lord – Rom 8:39, Counselor and Prince of peace – Isa 9:6, ...)

The case with John is parallel. This is Hayden's point. Extending this, one could say that since the Bible itself uses other terms for Jesus and John, then it would also follow that the Bible conflicts with itself (given this law of exclusion), and thus the Bible could not be the word of God. However, as shown in some detail in Chapter 22, the law of exclusion Hayden is using is false. Therefore, in fact, Mt 1:21 and Lk 1:13 do leave room for the other terms. Now, by refuting the *required specifics exclude* claim, has Hayden shown that *Bible silence forbids* is false? No.

No Relevance

If the Bible silence forbids doctrine were the same as this law of exclusion, or at least if it depended on its being true, **then** by refuting this so-called law, Hayden would be successfully refuting Bible silence forbids. But he and others have incorrectly assumed this equivalence or dependence.

Some silence forbids defenders have helped him think this way. This is seen in a 1970 editorial Hayden wrote in the *Christian Standard* in which he quotes from a 1969 *Firm Foundation* editorial by Reuel Lemmons. The two editors are referring to a meeting in St. Louis, MO between "members of the conservative Christian Church and the churches of Christ." Notice Hayden's quote of Lemmons:

> I felt that our main contention was that the Word of God is exclusive as well as inclusive in nature, and that the very commanding of a thing excluded all else.[136]

And,

> We pointed out that the Holy Spirit himself used these very arguments in Hebrews 1 and in Hebrews 7 to establish the superiority of Jesus over angels and to establish the priesthood of Christ as different from the priesthood of Aaron.[137]

So, for example, Lemmons is claiming Heb 7:13-14 is an instance of the required-specifics excludes "law." He is claiming that specifying the tribe of Levi is what excluded the tribe of Judah. (Actually, it was silence about Judah which excluded Judah. See Chapters 15 through 17.) Later in his editorial, while continuing to discuss this matter, Hayden refers to what Lemmons says as the silence forbids doctrine:

> The fact is that exclusion-by-silence is a principle that cannot be, and certainly has not been, applied consistently to Christian life and worship.[138]

But there is no logical connection between (1) Bible silence forbids and (2) A required specific excludes all other specifics on its level. Their meanings do not overlap. Quite to the contrary, silence is where there is **nothing** in the Bible on an action. But the *required specifics exclude* law claims there is **something** in the Bible regarding an action:

---

[136] Hayden, p. 3.
[137] Hayden, p. 3.
[138] Hayden, p. 3.

160

Namely the specific itself which allegedly **implies** the denial of that other action. But if there is Bible silence on a particular action, then there is no passage to which you can point having anything to do with that action, explicitly, implicitly, requiring, forbidding or permitting the action. (After determining there is silence, then you should go to the Bible silence forbids passages and conclude **from these** that the action is forbidden.) The moment you point to a passage which you claim deals with the particular action in question (including implied prohibition), then you are claiming there is something and not nothing, **not silence**.

So we have two different laws of exclusion here. They are different as seen by the fact that they have different starting points and bases: *Bible silence forbids* starts with nothing on a subject and then says the Bible teaches when there is nothing we are not to do the action (Heb 7:13-14; ...). But *required specifics exclude* starts with something, namely the required specific itself in the Bible, and then says this implies the denial of the other specifics.

Since the two are different and independent of each other, the truth or falsity of one of these laws tells us nothing about the truth or falsity of the other. Therefore, Hayden is refuting a law of exclusion which is irrelevant to the Bible silence forbids doctrine.

Modern Things Forbidden?

Does not the view that Bible silence forbids imply that the use of all devices and the practice of all actions which were not known in the first century also are forbidden? For example, does this not force us to say that we must not use airplanes, television, modern medical techniques and all other post-first century discoveries?

161

No. This makes the mistake of including implication in the term Bible silence, and then saying Bible silence forbids. In this case, "Bible silence" **would** forbid all post-first century discoveries. But as shown in Part 2, this is not the "silence" which the Bible forbids. When we keep this in mind, then we can see that God's word does allow us to use such discoveries.

Here are some passages which provide high enough generic authority to cover modern devices, except of course for any activity which the Bible elsewhere denies.

1 Tim 5:8:
> But if anyone does not provide for his own, and especially for those of his household, he has denied the faith and is worse than an unbeliever.

1 Tim 4:8:
> For bodily exercise profits a little, but godliness is profitable for all things, having promise of the life that now is and of that which is to come.

Mk 16:15-16:
> And He said to them, ''Go into all the world and preach the gospel to every creature. [16]''He who believes and is baptized will be saved; but he who does not believe will be condemned.''

Of further interest along these lines would be a study of "rest" (*anapauo* in the Greek) in Mk 6:31 as well as the meaning of subduing the earth in Gen 1:26-28. A discussion item at the end of the book invites the reader to study these.

Mk 6:31:

And He said to them, "Come aside by yourselves to a deserted place and rest a while." For there were many coming and going, and they did not even have time to eat.

Gen 1:26-28 with Heb 2:5-8:

Gen:

Then God said, 'Let Us make man in Our image, according to Our likeness; let them have dominion over the fish of the sea, over the birds of the air, and over the cattle, over all the earth and over every creeping thing that creeps on the earth.' [27]So God created man in His *own* image; in the image of God He created him; male and female He created them. [28]Then God blessed them, and God said to them, 'Be fruitful and multiply; fill the earth and subdue it; have dominion over the fish of the sea, over the birds of the air, and over every living thing that moves on the earth.'

Heb:

[5] For He has not put the world to come, of which we speak, in subjection to angels. [6] But one testified in a certain place, saying: "What is man that You are mindful of him, Or the son of man that You take care of him? [7]You have made him a little lower than the angels; You have crowned him with glory and honor, And set him over the works of Your hands. [8]You have put all things in subjection under his feet." For in that He put all in subjection under him, He left nothing *that is* not put under him. But now we do not yet see all things put under him.

(For an explanation of the last sentence in Heb 2:8, compare Rom 8:18-23 and 1 Cor 15:24-26.)

Paralyzed into Non-action?

Given the Bible silence forbids doctrine, wouldn't or shouldn't we be paralyzed into non-action, even regarding such daily activities as walking, until we find an okay from the Bible? Also, surely you are not telling us that every possible action we do must have an okay from the Bible. Does this not force you into the obvious error that the Bible has how-to instructions for everything?

First, it is not **necessary** to find an okay from the Bible to do daily activities such as walking. And this fact does not conflict with the inclusive language of 2 Tim 3:16-17, 1 Thes 5:21 and Col 3:17. This is so because we learn some things from observation of God's natural world. Bible revelation reveals all good works but natural revelation reveals some good works too. I heard a person explain that drilling into cement, to be effective, requires a drill RPM slower than drilling into other materials. Someone learned this by observing God's laws of physics in action. We learn some things that way. Can we learn God's will that way? On some things yes.

For example, we can tell from the appearance and usage of legs that they are at least for walking. Similarly, we can see God's intent for heterosexuality by comparing the sexual anatomies of the human male and the human female. Since the Bible contains all good works, all things which pertain to life and godliness, then we can correctly conclude that every good behavior discernible from nature is repeated in the Bible. But it is not necessary to wait for Bible study to engage in that which we can discern from God's book of nature. If you know the will of God on a matter, you know the will of God on that matter. Therefore, it is not the case that the Bible's silence forbids doctrine impractically paralyzes a person's choices to get on

164

with many of the activities of daily life. But regarding any action for which you cannot discern his will from nature, you do need to study the all-sufficient Bible. Such concern about God's will itself ought to be a part of our lives on earth. See the principle in 2 Tim 2:15.[139]

Second, Jesus said the Holy Spirit would teach **all** truth (Jn 16:13). Peter spoke of **all** things which pertain to life and godliness (2 Pet 1:3). These are equal to the *all* in the above referenced passages. The language in the referenced passages **is** inclusive language. Where's the "some" ?

Third, the passages do not teach that the Scriptures equip us unto every how-to instruction but unto every good work. If it's good, it is covered by the Bible somewhere as either an explicit or implicit requirement or permission. But as to how to do it, you may be on your own – with nature only. For example, I cannot go to the Bible to find source data for writing the present technical writing effort I am working on, *Installation and Maintenance of the TS50 Tool Monitoring* system. I have to ask the design engineer how he, so to speak, "subdued the earth" sufficiently to develop this product. But I can go the Bible to find out whether or not any work I do is good. 1 Tim 5:8 tells me I am doing a good work when writing the *TS50 I&M* document.

Fourth, consider the sinlessness of the incarnated Christ documented in the Bible. Does the Bible here, in one fell swoop, authorize day-to-day activities of the human body? The Bible does cover every good work. If it's good, it's in there, taught somewhere either explicitly or implicitly: 2 Tim 3:16-17.

---

[139] 2 Tim 2:15 (See page 4.)

Chapter 20
Bible Silence Permits
Claims (3)

Some claim there are Bible examples of human actions which God never authorized yet He approves of them. It is true that such an example would indeed teach that Bible silence permits. This is the case because all Bible-silent actions are Bible-unauthorized actions. So if one can show that Bible-unauthorized actions are permitted, then he has shown that Bible-silent actions must also be permitted. Also, such an example would deny Bible silence forbids, since the same action cannot be permitted by a being who knows all and never lies and simultaneously be forbidden by Him.

But are there such examples? Here are ten alleged. Let us see.

- Mt 4:23 (The Synagogue)
- Acts 6-7 (Stephen's Preaching)
- Mk 14:3-8 (The Woman Who Anointed Jesus)
- Mt 2:1-2, 9-12 (The Wise Men)
- Mt 8:2-3 (The Leper)
- Mk 5:22-23 (The Synagogue Ruler)
- Mt 15:21-28 (The Canaanite Woman)
- Lk 7:36-50 (The Woman Who Tended Jesus)
- Mk 10:46-52 (Blind Bartemaeus)
- Mt 28:6-10 (The Women from the Tomb)

166

Mt 4:23
(The Synagogue)

It is claimed that the OT scriptures are silent about the synagogue. Yet, there are passages like Mt 4:23 in which the sinless Jesus approved of the synagogue. Therefore, this reasoning continues, God's silence permits (and BSF must be false).

The passage reads,

> And Jesus went about all Galilee, teaching in their synagogues, preaching the gospel of the kingdom, and healing all kinds of sickness and all kinds of disease among the people. (Mt 4:23)

As we examine this argument, it is helpful first to observe the two parts of the word synagogue. It is composed of the Greek words *sun* (**pronounced** "soon" but **meaning** "with") and *ago* (pronounced "**ah** go" meaning "to go"). So, "to go with." The idea is a gathering of people, an assembly, and then the place where the assembly occurred, the building. Did the OT authorize assembling in a building for the activities in which Jesus and others engaged? It does and therefore the synagogue is **not** an example of silence.

To show this all we need to do is find an OT passage or combination of passages which **requires** the kinds of actions that were performed in a synagogue. We could look for passages which have to do with assembling or public teaching. To find these, one might want to start by looking up in a concordance terms like "gather," "law," "covenant," "children."

167

Here are two passages from the Psalms:

> Gather My saints together to Me, Those who have made a covenant with Me by sacrifice. (Ps 50:5)

> Give ear, O my people, *to* my law; Incline your ears to the words of my mouth. (Ps 78:1)

Here we have explicit authority for assembling, and implicit authority for a building. The explicit authority is in Ps 50:5. The implicit authority is shown by the fact that the instruction to gather and teach evident in both passages requires **some** place where this can be done. That is, due to the physical characteristics of this time-space-material world where God has placed humans, it is absolutely impossible to do the gathering and teaching which these passages **require**, and for there not to be some place in which to do them. Since the passages require a place, then they imply a place. Somebody's house is a place. Even the outside is some place. Standing in a field is some place. Being where there is light is some place. Being where there is not a blizzard is some place. The passages thus **imply** being at some physical place. And, as shown in Part 2 of this book, **implication is not silence.** A building like a synagogue is some place, which the OT does not condemn. So, we have shown that the OT is **not** silent on the synagogue. Therefore, the silence permits defender who appeals to the synagogue to prove his case is not providing an example of Bible silence.

Acts 6-7
(Stephen's Preaching)

Hayden claims that the following example disproves Bible silence forbids (and, one could add, proves BSP). He writes,

> Prohibition-by-silence would have established a double barrier against the short preaching career of Stephen (Acts 6 and 7). He was not among the apostles when Jesus commanded *them* to preach [Mt 28:18-20). He was chosen by the church and commissioned by the apostles to "serve tables" while the apostles gave themselves "to prayer and to the ministry of the word." This "deacon" very boldly went beyond his specific authorization, but the Holy Spirit still empowered his preaching.[140]

Hayden fails to see the difference between implication and silence. There is implied authority built into the great commission for Stephen's preaching.

The passage reads,

> [18] And Jesus came and spoke to them, saying, "All authority has been given to Me in heaven and on earth. [19] "Go therefore and make disciples of all the nations, baptizing them in the name of the Father and of the Son and of the Holy Spirit, [20] "teaching them to observe all things that I have commanded you; and lo, I am with you always, *even* to the end of the age." (Mt 28:18-20)

---

[140] Hayden, pp. 5-6.

169

Jesus tells his audience that they are to teach all nations to observe all things that he commanded them. Since he said "**all** things," then he includes the instruction in **this** passage to teach the gospel. Further, since he says "all the nations," he includes Stephen. So this great commission authorizes Stephen's action and thus the Bible is not silent on that action. Hayden's example (Stephen's preaching) is not an example of Bible silence. He has made the mistake of calling an implied action a Bible-silent action, and therefore his example has no relevance to silence. By pointing to Stephen, Hayden has neither disproved Bible silence forbids nor proved Bible silence permits.

MK14:3-8
(The Woman Who Annointed Jesus)

Blakely said,

> There are a number of incidents in Scripture where people are said to have worshiped our Lord Jesus Christ .... On one occasion a woman came in to our Lord, and without any authority whatsoever, without any Scriptural precedent, broke an alabaster box of ointment and poured it upon our Lord in honor and devotion to Him. While His disciples raised their ire because of this, He said, "Let her alone; she hath done a good deed. Wherever the gospel is preached this shall be made mention of her" – no authorization whatsoever, no precedent whatsoever.[141]

---

[141] Blakely, p. 39.

The passage reads,

> [3] And being in Bethany at the house of Simon the leper, as He sat at the table, a woman came having an alabaster flask of very costly oil of spikenard. Then she broke the flask and poured *it* on His head. [4] But there were some who were indignant among themselves, and said, "Why was this fragrant oil wasted? [5] "For it might have been sold for more than three hundred denarii and given to the poor." And they criticized her sharply. [6] But Jesus said, "Let her alone. Why do you trouble her? She has done a good work for Me. [7] "For you have the poor with you always, and whenever you wish you may do them good; but Me you do not have always. [8] "She has done what she could. She has come beforehand to anoint My body for burial. [9] "Assuredly, I say to you, wherever this gospel is preached in the whole world, what this woman has done will also be told as a memorial to her. (Mk 14:3-9)

To begin with, where is worship in the passage? In verse 6, in response to the charge that she could have helped the poor instead, Jesus calls her action a good work. "For" in verse 7 signals He is going to explain what He means. In His explanation, Jesus grants that helping the poor is a good work, but explains that helping Him also is a good work. He thus categorizes her behavior in the area of benevolence. In verse 8, He even identifies the specific purpose of her action: To anoint His body for burial. Jesus was a worthy recipient of her benevolence:

> [7] He was oppressed and He was afflicted,
> .... [8] ... He was cut off from the land of the
> living; ....[9] And they made His grave with the
> wicked - But with the rich at His death, ...
> (Is 53:7-9)

> Foxes have holes and birds of the air *have*
> nests, but the Son of Man has nowhere to lay
> *His* head. (Mt 8:20)

Is there no Scriptural precedence for her behavior in the OT? Do we have OT Scripture which explicitly or implicitly covers what she did? Yes.

A relevant OT command:

> Do not withhold good from those to whom it
> is due, When it is in the power of your hand
> to do *so.*(Prov 3:27)

A relevant declarative statement in the OT, speaking of the poor:

> but you shall open your hand wide to him and
> willingly lend him sufficient for his need,
> whatever he needs. (Dt 15:8)

An approved example in the OT, which God obviously wanted emulated:

> Everyone helped his neighbor, And said to his brother, "Be of good courage." (Is 41:6)

So there are OT passages which cover what the woman did.

Blakely refers to more alleged examples of unauthorized yet approved behavior: He said,

> Do you not remember the wise men that came and worshiped Christ? They brought unto Him *unauthorized* gifts: gold, frankincense and myrrh. They were not told to do it. The leper who came to Jesus and made an unauthorized request – it says he worshiped Him, making this request: "If thou wilt, thou canst make me clean." A certain ruler came to Jesus with an unauthorized request, saying, "My daughter lieth near death, come and lay thy hand upon her." Unauthorized, yet the Holy Spirit said he worshiped Jesus when he said it. The unauthorized woman of Canaan, an unauthorized person with an unauthorized request: "Lord, help me!" She went away that day having worshiped the Lord Jesus Christ .... [142]

Let us examine these in the order in which he mentions them.

---

[142] Blakely, p. 46.

Mt 2.1-2, 9-12
(The Wise Men)

This passage reads,

> [1] Now after Jesus was born in Bethlehem of Judea in the days of Herod the king, behold, wise men from the East came to Jerusalem, [2] saying, "Where is He who has been born King of the Jews? For we have seen His star in the East and have come to worship Him." ... [11] And when they had come into the house, they saw the young Child with Mary His mother, and fell down and worshiped Him. And when they had opened their treasures, they presented gifts to Him: gold, frankincense, and myrrh. [12] Then, being divinely warned in a dream that they should not return to Herod, they departed for their own country another way.

First, how does this show either that Bible silence forbids does not apply today in the Christian age, or that Bible silence permits does apply today? The individuals referenced in the above passage appear to be gentiles, not Jews. To show Bible silence forbids, why am I compelled to show OT Scripture for all acts of **gentile** worship before the Christian age? As was shown in Chapter 17, the book of Hebrews establishes that the silence forbids doctrine is true of both the OT and the NT. The NT has a universal scope (Mt 28:18-20). Though there are references to gentiles in the OT, nevertheless its scope is not as broad as that of the NT. The Bible says, to the Jews "were committed the oracles of God." (Rom 3:1-2). The gentiles are said to be those "who do not have the law" (Rom 2:14). The basis of judgment for gentiles who lived during OT times will

174

overlap with that of the Jews, but there are differences (Rom 2:12-16). They had law because all are sinners. However, as shown below, this particular case of the wise men is sufficiently covered in the OT. But if it had not been, this would not have established that the silence forbids doctrine did not apply in OT times or does not apply in NT times.

Second, the passage tells us the wise men worshiped Jesus. But the passage is sparse in detail, except that verse 11 says they fell down. So they worshiped in some posture which resulted from that. We do have OT passages which speak of such posture in worship:

> "… they bowed their faces to the ground on the pavement, and worshiped and praised the LORD, …." (2 Chron 7:3)

> And Jehoshaphat bowed his head with *his* face to the ground, and all Judah and the inhabitants of Jerusalem bowed before the LORD, worshiping the LORD. (2 Chron 20:18)

> [24] You have been rebellious against the LORD from the day that I knew you. [25] Thus I prostrated myself before the LORD; forty days and forty nights I kept prostrating myself, because the LORD had said He would destroy you. [26] Therefore I prayed to the LORD ….[1] At that time the LORD said to me, 'Hew for yourself two tablets of stone like the first, and come up to Me on the mountain and make yourself an ark of wood.' (Dt 9:24-10:1)

175

Third, even though OT legislation had limited scope as shown above, it does provide information which covers the wise men event of Mt 2. In the following two passages, notice especially the generic "all nations shall serve him" (Ps 72:10), and the generic "The wealth of the Gentiles shall come to you" (Is 60:6).

> The kings of Tarshish and of the isles will bring presents; the kings of Sheba and Seba will offer gifts. Yes, all kings shall fall down before Him; all nations shall serve Him. (Ps 72:10)

> (5) ... The wealth of the Gentiles shall come to you. (6) The multitude of camels shall cover your *land*, the dromedaries of Midian and Ephah; all those from Sheba shall come; they shall bring gold and incense, and they shall proclaim the praises of the LORD. (Is 60:5-6)

So, with his reference to the wise men, Blakely is mistaken. The event proves nothing about the application of Bible silence forbids in our day. And, as it turns out, the OT does address their behavior.

Mt 8:2-4
(The Leper)

Blakely said, "The leper who came to Jesus and made an unauthorized request – it says he worshiped Him, making this request: 'If thou wilt, thou canst make me clean."

This passage reads,

> [2] And behold, a leper came and worshiped Him, saying, "Lord, if You are willing, You can make me clean." [3] Then Jesus put out *His* hand and touched him, saying, "I am willing; be cleansed." Immediately his leprosy was cleansed. [4] And Jesus said to him, "See that you tell no one; but go your way, show yourself to the priest, and offer the gift that Moses commanded, as a testimony to them."

First, did not the OT authorize the people to worship deity, praising the Lord's capability and asking the capable God for a blessing which God was willing to give? There appears to be a need to become more familiar with the OT, or to understand better how implication works: How meanings of passages include specific actions. One is reminded of a statement made in another context at Mt 9:13, "But go and learn what *this* means ...." In fact, it would be instructive to look up "mean" in a Bible concordance and notice how this term includes implications: What this means - That is, What does the passage include? What are some of the specifics implied?

Second, note the wording of Mt 8 above as to what the leper did, and observe the following practices reflected in OT Scriptures:

> Give unto the LORD the glory due to His name; Worship the LORD in the beauty of holiness. (Ps 29:2).

> "... they ... worshiped and praised the LORD, ..." (2 Chron 7:3)

> "... The hand of our God *is* upon all those for good who seek Him, but His power and His wrath *are* against all those who forsake Him." [23] So we fasted and entreated our God for this, and He answered our prayer...." (Ezra 8:22)

Third, why do not the OT passages on prayer cover the leper's behavior? Legion are the OT passages on prayer, as an avenue for praising God and asking Him for a blessing. It is true that one could point to Jn 14:13-14 and 15:16, where Jesus speaks of asking the Father for blessings through His (Jesus') name. But in those passages, Jesus is giving instruction to His disciples about future prayer activity. Here in Mt 8 we have a Jew, living during OT times (Gal 4:4; Heb 9:16-17), asking God incarnate for a blessing (Jn 1:1-14).

Fourth, in Mt 8:4, Jesus instructed the leper to go to the priest. This shows Jesus' insistence that the leper's behavior be within the confines of OT legislation. Mt 8:4, then, should have given Blakely the hint that one could find the OT passages which we did find in covering the leper's actions in Mt 8:1-3.

What we have said in response to Blakely's preceding claims adequately answers his claims about the synagogue ruler, the Canaanite woman and the woman who tended Jesus. So I will cite these passages here and let the reader make analysis. I **will** examine the account of the woman who tended Jesus, and Blakely's additional thoughts on that passage.

Mk 5.22-23
(The Synagogue Ruler)

[22] And behold, one of the rulers of the synagogue came, Jairus by name. And when he saw Him, he fell at His feet [23] and begged Him earnestly, saying, "My little daughter lies at the point of death. Come and lay Your hands on her, that she may be healed, and she will live."

Mt 15.21-28
(The Canaanite Woman)

[21] Then Jesus went out from there and departed to the region of Tyre and Sidon. [22] And behold, a woman of Canaan came from that region and cried out to Him, saying, "Have mercy on me, O Lord, Son of David! My daughter is severely demon-possessed." [23] But He answered her not a word. And His disciples came and urged Him, saying, "Send her away, for she cries out after us." [24] But He answered and said, "I was not sent except to the lost sheep of the house of Israel." [25] Then she came and worshiped Him, saying, "Lord, help me!" [26] But He answered and said, "It is not good to take the children's bread and throw *it* to the little dogs." [27] And she said, "Yes, Lord, yet even the little dogs eat the crumbs which fall from their masters' table." [28] Then Jesus answered and said to her, "O woman, great *is* your faith! Let it be to you as you desire." And her daughter was healed from that very hour.

Lk 7:36-50
(The Woman Who Tended Jesus)

[36] Then one of the Pharisees asked Him to eat with him. And He went to the Pharisee's house, and sat down to eat. [37] And behold, a woman in the city who was a sinner, when she knew that *Jesus* sat at the table in the Pharisee's house, brought an alabaster flask of fragrant oil, [38] and stood at His feet behind *Him* weeping; and she began to wash His feet with her tears, and wiped *them* with the hair of her head; and she kissed His feet and anointed *them* with the fragrant oil. [39] Now when the Pharisee who had invited Him saw *this,* he spoke to himself, saying, "This man, if He were a prophet, would know who and what manner of woman *this is* who is touching Him, for she is a sinner." [40] And Jesus answered and said to him, "Simon, I have something to say to you." So he said, "Teacher, say it." [41] "There was a certain creditor who had two debtors. One owed five hundred denarii, and the other fifty. [42] "And when they had nothing with which to repay, he freely forgave them both. Tell Me, therefore, which of them will love him more?" [43] Simon answered and said, "I suppose the *one* whom he forgave more." And He said to him, "You have rightly judged." [44] Then He turned to the woman and said to Simon, "Do you see this woman? I entered your house; you gave Me no water for My feet, but she has washed My feet with her tears and wiped *them* with the hair of her head. [45] "You gave Me no kiss, but this woman has not ceased to kiss My feet since the time I came in. [46] "You did not anoint My head with oil, but this woman has anointed My feet with fragrant oil. [47] "Therefore I say to you, her sins, *which are* many, are forgiven,

for she loved much. But to whom little is forgiven, *the same* loves little." [48] Then He said to her, "Your sins are forgiven." [49] And those who sat at the table with Him began to say to themselves, "Who is this who even forgives sins?" [50] Then He said to the woman, "Your faith has saved you. Go in peace." (Lk 7:36-50)

To Lk 7, Blakely adds a part of Rom 14. He said,

The Word of God says that the kingdom of God is *not* in meat or drink, but in righteousness and peace and joy in the Holy Spirit, for he that in these things ... serveth Christ is acceptable to God and approved of men. ... Why *did* Jesus receive that alabaster box? ... Why did He let the woman wash His feet with her tears and dry them with her hair? Why did He? It was not authorized. Why did He receive it? He that in these things – righteousness, peace and joy in the Holy Spirit – serves Him is accepted. [143]

His reference to Rom 14, with some additional context, reads,

[14] I know and am convinced by the Lord Jesus that *there is* nothing unclean of itself; but to him who considers anything to be unclean, to him *it is* unclean. [15] Yet if your brother is grieved because of *your* food, you are no longer walking in love. Do not destroy with your food the one for whom Christ

---

[143] Blakely, p. 64.

died. [16] Therefore do not let your good be spoken of as evil; [17] for the kingdom of God is not eating and drinking, but righteousness and peace and joy in the Holy Spirit. [18] For he who serves Christ in these things *is* acceptable to God and approved by men. [19] Therefore let us pursue the things *which make* for peace and the things by which one may edify another. [20] Do not destroy the work of God for the sake of food. All things indeed *are* pure, but *it is* evil for the man who eats with offense. (Rom 14:14-20)

First, Blakely cites Lk 7 as an example of unauthorized yet acceptable behavior, and then cites the Rom 14:17 principle as proof it was authorized! With the first half of this claim, he asserts that the actions in Lk 7 constitute an example of Bible silence permits. With the last half, he asserts Rom 14:17 **implies** that the actions in Lk 7 are acceptable. This is an implication claim, not a silence claim. So with one hand Blakely attempts to give us an example of Bible silence. But with the other, he himself takes it away.

Second, I agree there is implied Biblical authority for the events of Lk 7. To show this, I call attention to the same kind of OT passages which refute Blakely's foregoing claims. Further, I do believe we can find principles in the OT which overlap with Rom 14:17. But since Lk 7 happened during OT times, a more direct way of showing authority for the woman's behavior is to start and end with the OT. So I refer the reader to the OT passages which refute Blakely's foregoing claims.

Third, to understand Rom 14, one needs to read the whole chapter. Without delving into a thorough-going exegesis here, I will provide this summary. Paul is talking about whether or not it is permissible to eat meat. The passage teaches eating meat is optional. The doubters, because they **are** in doubt, are in no position to condemn the behavior of the non-doubters. And the non-doubters must not condemn the doubters, for the doubters are not sinning by not engaging in an optional action. Further, the non-doubters must not force the doubters to do that which, as far as they know at present, may very well be sinful. Verse 17, to which Blakely refers us, should be understood in this context: Exercise the indicated tolerance toward one another regarding the eating of food or drink There is righteousness on both sides here. So, though you differ, you should be able to attain the peace and joy, as well as the righteousness, which characterize the kingdom of God.

Mk 10.46-52
(Blind Bartemaeus)

Blakely adds Mk 10. He writes,

Blind Bartemaeus – thank God he didn't know about this rule that says you cannot offer something or come to Him without being authorized. He would have never been healed of his blindness. "Jesus, thou Son of David, have mercy on me!" His action was unauthorized, but he came away healed, because he approached in spirit and in Truth – in comportment with reality.[144]

---

[144] Blakely, p. 66.

This passage reads,

> [46] Now they came to Jericho. As He went out of Jericho with His disciples and a great multitude, blind Bartimaeus, the son of Timaeus, sat by the road begging. [47] And when he heard that it was Jesus of Nazareth, he began to cry out and say, "Jesus, Son of David, have mercy on me!" [48] Then many warned him to be quiet; but he cried out all the more, "Son of David, have mercy on me!" [49] So Jesus stood still and commanded him to be called. Then they called the blind man, saying to him, "Be of good cheer. Rise, He is calling you." [50] And throwing aside his garment, he rose and came to Jesus. [51] So Jesus answered and said to him, "What do you want Me to do for you?" The blind man said to Him, "Rabboni, that I may receive my sight." [52] Then Jesus said to him, "Go your way; your faith has made you well." And immediately he received his sight and followed Jesus on the road.

What we have said in response to Blakely's preceding claims adequately answers his claims about Bartemaeus and the women from the tomb.

Mt 28.6-10
(The Women from the Tomb)

Blakely adds an alleged example from Mt 28. He said,

How about the women who met Jesus when He was coming away from the tomb? They held Him by the feet and worshiped Him, the Scripture says. Completely unauthorized they were, yet the Lord Jesus did not turn them away.[145]

This passage reads,

[6] "He is not here; for He is risen, as He said. Come, see the place where the Lord lay. [7] "And go quickly and tell His disciples that He is risen from the dead, and indeed He is going before you into Galilee; there you will see Him. Behold, I have told you." [8] So they went out quickly from the tomb with fear and great joy, and ran to bring His disciples word. [9] And as they went to tell His disciples, behold, Jesus met them, saying, "Rejoice!" So they came and held Him by the feet and worshiped Him. [10] Then Jesus said to them, "Do not be afraid. Go *and* tell My brethren to go to Galilee, and there they will see Me." (Mt 28:6-10)

As mentioned, see the preceding analyses for adequate treatment of Blakely's claims here.

This ends our analysis of various attempts to deny Bible silence forbids or affirm Bible silence permits. Since the Bible does not conflict with itself, then we expect that no Bible teaching denies that its silence forbids.

---

[145] Blakely, p. 66.

Part 3:
Related Topics

There are several topics relevant to what we discussed in Parts 1 and 2, which I did not address there. This is the reason for Part 3. Each of these is related either to the study of implication, to the study of silence or both.

Chapter 21
Other BSF Passages

There are other passages offered in support of Bible silence forbids in addition to those given in Chapters 15 through 17. In this chapter we discuss some of these, although we will not attempt to provide an exhaustive list.

Do Not Add To or Take Away From
Several passages teach we are not to add to or take away from God's word.

Rev 22:18-19 reads:

> [18]For I testify to everyone who hears the words of the prophecy of this book: If anyone adds to these thing, God will add to him the plagues that are written in this book; [19]and if anyone takes away from the words of the book of this prophecy, God shall take away his part from the Book of Life, from the holy city, and *from* the things which are written in this book.

Starting with Silence-Permits
We have already shown that the silence of the Bible forbids. Hold this in suspension for the moment and let us see how Rev 22:18-19 deals with the question of how to interpret the Bible's silence. Suppose a person comes along who is a *silence permits* defender. He claims that the Bible teaches in passage X that its silence permits. You call his attention to Rev

22:18-19 as proof that the silence of the Bible forbids. You stress the *do not add to* part of the passage, pointing out that he should not add a permission where the Bible does not give one. This gentleman responds saying that these two Bible teachings, the Rev 22:18-19 teaching and the X teaching, are compatible. "The Bible teaches in passage X that its silence permits," he points out. "So," he continues, "when someone goes ahead and performs an action about which the Bible is silent, he is not at all adding to or taking away from the Bible, for the Bible itself teaches that he has permission to do the action. "Further," he observes, "if **you** teach that a person is forbidden to perform an action about which the Bible is silent, **it is you** who would be violating Rev 22:18-19. This is the case because you would be **taking away** passage X, thus violating the second part of Rev 22:18-19. And you would be **adding** the unsupported teaching that silence forbids, thus violating the first part of Rev 22:18-19."

Starting with Silence-Forbids

On the other hand, now suppose a person comes along who is a *silence forbids* defender. He claims that the Bible teaches in passage X that its silence forbids. You call his attention to Rev 22:18-19 as proof that the silence of the Bible permits. You stress the *do not take away from* part of the passage, pointing out that he should not remove a permission where the Bible gives one. This gentleman responds saying that these two Bible teachings, the Rev 22:18-19 teaching and the X teaching, are compatible. "The Bible teaches in passage X that its silence forbids," he points out. "So," he continues, "when someone goes ahead and performs an action about which the Bible is silent, he is adding to and taking away from the Bible, for the Bible itself teaches that he is forbidden to do such an action. "Further," he observes, "if **you** teach that a person is permitted to perform an action about which the Bible is silent, **it is you** who would be violating Rev 22:18-19. This is

188

the case because you would be **taking away** passage X, thus violating the second part of Rev 22:18-19. And you would be **adding** the unsupported teaching that silence permits, thus violating the first part of Rev 22:18-19."

Who Does Not Violate Rev 22:18-19?
The one who can produce passage X. If there is no passage which supports the view, there is no Biblical basis for so explaining Rev 22:18-19. But the silence-forbids defender can produce such a passage as we have shown. The *silence permits* defender cannot. Therefore, indeed, it is the *silence permits* defender who is violating Rev 22:18-19 in that he is taking away Col 3:17, 2 Tim 3:16-17 with 1 Th 5:21 and the Hebrews passages, which **are** in the Bible. This is thus violating the second part of Rev 22:18-19 (do not take away from). Also, he is adding to the Bible *the silence permits* doctrine, which is nowhere in the Bible. This is thus violating the first part of Rev 22:18-19 (do not add to).

Each individual in the foregoing discussions starts with the view that the Bible teaches his view in some passage (X). There is another starting point we sometimes hear. Some hold that there is no passage in the Bible teaching either the *silence forbids* doctrine or the *silence permits* doctrine. Some conclude from this claim that we can do the action or not do it with God's approval. But this is claiming that since the Bible teaches neither *silence forbids* nor *silence permits*, then silence permits. This is self-contradictory and therefore false.

Other *Do Not Add To* Passages
We have seen then that it is the *silence permits* defender who violates the Rev 22:18-19 principle. On the same reasoning, he violates any other passage which teaches what Rev 22:18-19 teaches. Let us say a bit more about these verses and then list other such passages.

It does appear that Rev 22:18-19 is referring directly to the book of Revelation. There are several indications of this. *First,* notice it is "this" book in the two verses: "this book" and "the words of the prophesy of this book" (the Greek demonstrative pronoun of nearness, *houtos*). Notice 22:7, 9 and 10 which also speak of "this book." *Second,* verses 18 and 19 refer to subjects all of which the book of Revelation addresses, but which some other Bible books do not address: plagues (9:20; 11:6; 15:1, 6, 8; 16:9, 21; 18:4, 8; 21:9), tree of life (2:7; 22:2, 14), the holy city (11:2; 21:2, 10, and described throughout chapter 21 and at 22:14).

But the principle of not adding to or taking away from applies to the rest of the Bible too. This follows from the fact that the Bible, all of the Bible together, is God's all-sufficient revelation. Therefore, one should not add to or take away from any of it. Since it is God's word, we should not change any of its ingredients.

From the foregoing reasoning, then, we conclude that the *silence permits* doctrine does violate every passage which contains the same principle as Rev 22:18-19.

Dt 4:2:

> 'You shall not add to the word which I command you, nor take from it, that you may keep the commandments of the Lord you God which I command you.

Dt 12:32:

> 'Whatever I command you, be careful to observe it; you shall not add to it nor take away from it.

Josh 1:7 (ASV):

> 'Only be strong and very courageous, that you may observe to do according to all the law which Moses My servant commanded you; do not turn from it to the right hand or to the left, that you may prosper wherever you go.

Prov 30:6:

> Do not add to His words, Lest He rebuke you, and you be found a liar.

1 Cor 4:6:

> Now these things, brethren, I have figuratively transferred to myself and Apollos for your sakes, that you may learn in us not to think beyond what is written, that none of you may be puffed up on behalf of one against the other.

2 Jn 9:

> Whoever transgresses and does not abide in the doctrine of Christ does not have God. He who abides in the doctrine of Christ has both the Father and the Son.

More Passages

Here are additional passages to consider in defense of BSF.

2 Cor 5:7a with Rom 10:17

2 Cor 5:7a:

> For we walk by faith, not by sight.

Rom 10:17:

> So then faith comes by hearing, and hearing by the word of God.

So we are to walk by faith (2 Cor 5:7a) and faith comes from hearing the word of God (Rom 10:17). If the Bible is silent regarding an action, then a person cannot hear about that action from the word of God. And if a person cannot hear about that action from the word of God, then he cannot have the Rom 10:17 kind of faith (confidence) in that action. And if a person cannot have the Rom 10:17 kind of faith in an action, then he cannot do that action in the way 2 Cor 5:7a speaks. Thus, if the Bible is silent regarding an action, we ought not do that action.

Jn 4:24 with 17:17 (Regarding Worship)
'God *is* Spirit, and those who worship Him must worship in spirit and truth.' (Jn 4:24)

'Sanctify them by Your truth. Your word is truth. (Jn 17:17)

We must worship in spirit and in truth (Jn 4:24). God's word is truth (Jn 17:17). So we must worship according to God's word. But if God's word is silent on an act of worship, then we cannot engage in that act of worship in truth. Therefore, Bible silence on worship forbids.

Mk 7:7-9

[7]And in vain they worship Me, Teaching *as* doctrines the commandments of men.'[8] "For laying aside the commandment of God, you hold the tradition of men—the washing of pitchers and cups, and many other such things you do." [9] He said to them, "*All too* well you reject the commandment of God, that you may keep your tradition.

Here we have two sources of authority identified, God and man. Jesus rejects man as the source. But BSP endorses action whose source of authority is man and not God. This is so because when there is nothing in God's word regarding an act of worship, and you go ahead and do it, you do so without God's authority but man's only. The Bible silence permits doctrine thus bases action on authority Jesus rejects.

Chapter 22
What Does the
Forbidding?

The Bible excludes (that is, forbids) the use of instrumental music in Christian worship. But how the Bible does so is sometimes misunderstood. It is not the NT requirement *to sing* found in Col 3:16 and other passages which forbids the instrument. Rather, these passages themselves allow for another passage to authorize the instrument. The problem is that no other NT passage does this. The NT is silent on the use of a musical instrument in Christian worship. **This** is what forbids the instrument: The silence outlaws its use because the silence of the Bible forbids (Col 3:17[146]; ...). So it is passages like Col 3:**17** which forbid the instrument, not passages like Col 3:**16**.[147]

Roy Deaver correctly makes this distinction. He expresses it like this:

It is not at all my view that sing excludes play. Rather, it is my view that sing authorizes singing, and that this is all that it does.[148]

---

[146] Col 3:17 "And whatever you do in world or deed, *do* all in the name of the Lord Jesus, giving thanks to God the Father through Him."

[147] Col 3:16 "Let the word of Christ dwell in you richly in all wisdom, teaching and admonishing one another in psalms and hymns and spiritual songs, singing with grace in your hearts to the Lord."

[148] Roy Deaver, *The Problem with Instrumental Music* (Austin, TX: Biblical Notes, 1995), p. 63.

194

He continues,

> The excluding factor is the absence of authority.[149]

And,

> Playing (mechanical instrumental music in Christian worship) is excluded not by the command for us to sing, but by the fact that there is no authority for the playing.[150]

G. C. Brewer saw this. In his book, *A Medley on the Music Question* he defines several words:

> *Sing* – "To utter words or sounds musically or with melodious modulations of voice."
> *Include* – "To hold, contain, to confine within; to comprehend."
> *Exclude* – "To shut out, to except or reject."
> *Preclude* – "To close up, stop up, prevent access to; to prevent by anticipative action."
> *Interdict* – "To declare authoritatively against, as the use or doing of something; debar by forbidding; prohibit peremptorily."[151]

On the next page he makes these observations:

> *A word authorizes us to do only that which it includes in its meaning.*[152]

---

[149] Deaver, p. 63.
[150] Deaver, p. 63.
[151] G. C. Brewer, *A Medley on the Music Question or A Potpourri of Philology* (Nashville: Gospel Advocate Company, 1948), p. 61.

He continues,

> But a word may not – and in the music controversy
> the words used *do not* – *preclude* or *interdict* things
> that they do not *include*. Take the word "sing." By no
> manner of juggling words or of misrepresenting facts
> can we make that word *include* anything but vocal
> music – something done by the voice. It, therefore,
> *excludes*[153] instrumental music. It is not *included,* and,
> therefore, it is *left out.* So far as the word "sing" is
> concerned, there is no instrumental music in the thing
> described. But the word does not *preclude* or *debar*
> instrumental music. If any other command to use the
> instrument can be found, there will be no *conflict* or
> *contradiction* of the command by the other command –
> the one that says "sing." In the absence, however, of
> the second command, the instrument is *excluded* – *not
> authorized, left out.*[154]

---

[152] Brewer, p. 62.

[153] There are two meanings of *excludes* that are used when folks discuss this
subject. One is simply "not include," which is Brewer's meaning here. The
other is "forbids," or using Brewer's words from our footnote 151 quote,
"interdict." "Reject" in his definition of *excludes* in footnote 151 is this
second meaning. Roy Deaver uses *excludes* in this second sense in our
footnote 150 quote of him. Brewer seems to use the second meaning in the
last sentence of our footnote 154 quote of him. Not rightly dividing the two
meanings may be what has led some Bible students to affirm "to specify is to
exclude." See *Why the Confusion?* later in this chapter. For clarity, in this
chapter I sometimes place "forbids" in parentheses after *excludes* when using
the second meaning.

[154] Brewer, p. 62.

Then Brewer writes,

> This author might say: "I heard a mixed quartet *sing*, 'Lead, Kindly Light,' at William McKinley's funeral." Can anyone know from that statement whether the quartet sang *a capella* or whether there was instrumental accompaniment? What is your guess, dear reader? Now, if the word "sing" included instrumental music, there would be no guessing about it. You would *know* that such music was used. Or if the word "sing" *precluded* or *interdicted* instrumental music, there would be no guessing. You would know that it was *not used.* But since the word "sing" neither *includes* nor *precludes* the instrument, you cannot know whether or not such music was used at McKinley's funeral.[155]

James D. Bales saw this. His book on instrumental music has a section titled "Command To Sing Prohibit Playing?" in the chapter titled "The Silence of the Scriptures." Bales quotes the same definitions from Brewer as in our footnote 151 above. Then he writes:

> G. C. Brewer pointed out that a "word authorizes us to do only that which it includes in its meaning."[156]

---

[155] Brewer, p. 62.

[156] James D. Bales, *Instrumental Music and New Testament Worship* (Searcy, Arkansas: Resource Publications, 1973), p. 200.

Bales then says in his own words, though following Brewer:

> However, as we have shown, a word does not *preclude* or
> *interdict* things which it does not include. Sing includes singing
> and not instrumental music. However, if another command
> authorized instrumental music it would not be debarred by the
> command to sing.[157]

M. C. Kurfees saw this in some of his writings. And Kurfees' thoughts
to which I am referring are among quotations concerning which Foy E.
Wallace said, "We submit these articles in their present form with the firm
belief that a careful reading will prove of great benefit to all."[158] In Section
2 of his book on instrumental music, Wallace quotes articles by M. C.
Kurfees that had appeared in the Nashville periodical, the *Gospel
Advocate*, in 1917. One of these is a reply to a letter Kurfees received from
J. B. Briney. Notice Kurfees' words:

> 3. He says we claim "that one cannot use an instrument in
> connection with *psalloing* without transgressing the command (if
> command it be) to sing or *psallein*." Wrong again, dear brother.
> We make no such claim as "that one cannot use an instrument ...
> without transgressing the command to sing or *psallein*." We
> simply claim that *using an instrument* is not obeying the
> command that is in "psallo." "Psallo" means to *sing*, and singing
> is not *playing an instrument*. Playing instruments is no more a
> transgression of "the command to sing or *psallein*" than it is a
> transgression of the command to love one another," and neither is
> it *in* "the command to sing or *psallein*."[159]

Some Bible students miss this point altogether. Some are inconsistent
about it. They argue that the instruction *to sing* in Col 3:16 excludes
(forbids) playing the instrument in Christian worship. Similarly, some
argue that God's specifying to Noah to make the ark out of gopher wood
itself forbade the use of other kinds of wood as a substitution and as an
addition. This is incorrect. The errors stem from belief in a general rule of
which these are instances. The general rule, sometimes called "to specify is

---

[157] Bales, p. 200.
[158] Foy E. Wallace, Jr., *The Instrumental Music Question* (Fort Worth, TX:
Foy E. Wallace Jr. Publications, 1980), p. 29.
[159] Wallace, p. 58.

198

to exclude" is the problem, because it is false, as we shall see further. (It is false with one exception. This exception is mentioned in the next paragraph and on page 212.)

A person is correct in teaching that it would have been sinful for Noah to have built the whole ark or a part of the ark out of non-gopher wood. But the sinfulness has nothing to do with the fact that the non-gopher wood has a specific-to-specific relationship to gopher wood, under the same generic *wood*. It is thus not due to "to specify is to exclude." Rather, the sinfulness is due to the absence of authority (the absence of an affirmation) for the non-gopher wood. It was sinful to use non-gopher wood because God nowhere authorized non-gopher wood. This lack of authority is of two kinds: One kind forbade **substituting** non-gopher wood for gopher wood, and the other kind of the unauthorized forbade **adding** non-gopher wood to the gopher wood. Let's talk about these in turn. *First*, the **requirement** to use gopher wood forbade **substituting** non-gopher wood for the gopher wood. To require is to forbid anything that prevents the requirement. (*To require is thus to forbid*, not *to specify is to forbid*, unless by specify - and here is the exception – the reference is to a **required** specific. But even here it's the requirement not the specificity that is forbidding the substitution.) So building the **whole** ark out of non-gopher wood would have been wrong, because it substitutes and thus would have prevented doing the divine requirement. A requirement implicitly forbids anything that is substituted for it. So it is correct to say "To require is to forbid substitution." But what about additions, where you still have gopher wood, but you are including non-gopher wood? With a sustitution you do not have the gopher wood at all. But with an addition, you have gopher wood plus something else. Additions are forbidden not by the **requirement** (which only forbids substitutions) but by the silence.

Let us now turn to this *second* kind of the unauthorized. There was silence about using non-gopher wood. So building even **some** of the ark out of non-gopher was sinful, because God's silence forbids as we have shown in earlier chapters. Therefore, **adding** some wood to the gopher wood would also have been wrong. It was silence, and thus the lack of divine authority for adding any other kind of wood, which forbade adding any other kind of wood.

It is the requirement (the implied prohibition) that excluded (forbade) the non-gopher wood as a substitution and the silence that excluded (forbade) the non-gopher wood as addition(s). It was not the specificity under a generic that excluded non-gopher wood from righteousness. The claim that a statement forbids what in fact it does not forces us into errors, if we are consistent. Let me elaborate, by analyzing a book where "to specify is to exclude" is expressed and illustrated at length. In several other regards, the book is very good.

We Be Brethren by J. D. Thomas

The book I would like for us to examine is often quoted among us: *We Be Brethren* by J. D. Thomas, first published in 1958. Thomas discusses several matters, including what can be called laws of inclusion and exclusion. As I indicated above, some of what he says is fine.[160] But he expresses error on what does the excluding (forbidding),[161] as other writers sometimes do. Let's allow him to tell us using his own words and illustrations.

Under the heading *"The Interrelation of Generics, Specifics, and Expedients,"* he writes:

> The term "generic" means basically "of a genus" or *class.* To mention a class, therefore, such as "mammals," necessarily implies and includes all of the specifics or subgroups within the genus. Thus, an action, such as "Worship God," would be considered to be the *genus,* while all detailed acts of worship – for

---

[160] For example, notice this helpful definition of legalism to ponder: "An overconcern to the point that one 'makes laws' where God hasn't, because he feels that every detail must be covered by a sharply defined law, and generic authority alone is too vague for a secure feeling." J. D. Thomas, *We Be Brethren* (Abilene, Texas: Biblical Research Press, 1958), p. 252.

[161] I sent a letter to J. D. Thomas dated Feb 11, 1996 in which I explained my thinking and asked if he might want to revise his on what excludes. After a while he returned my letter with several hand-written comments on it. He indicated he still believes he is correct, and that I am mistaken. He said, "Gopher' both authorizes one kind of wood and excludes others by logical inference. You are trying to make a distinction where there is none, really." (His underline.) One part of my letter quotes the following statement by Roy Deaver (which I quoted earlier in this chapter): "… it is my view that sing authorizes singing and that this is all that it does." Thomas underlined "and that this is all that it does" and wrote "No." If he were only saying a divine **requirement** forbids all substitutions, there would be no objection from me. But to claim that to **specify** forbids substitutions and additions is incorrect. In all fairness, I want to point out that J. D. Thomas indicated in his reply that he was not in good health and reminded me he is 85 years old. I appreciate his graciousness in replying to me.

200

example, sing, pray, teach, commemorate the Lord's death, and have fellowship - are specifics to this *genus* and would be implied and included in it.

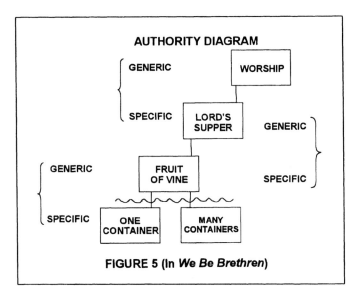

FIGURE 5 (In *We Be Brethren*)

In Figure 5, as far down the diagram as God has specified or *required* a certain matter, that item is obligatory upon us and is not optional. But in the point of such a scale of relationship where God stops specifying what man must do, there we draw our "wavy line" and we understand that all relationships below this point are optional matters ....[162]

Under the heading *"Excluded Matters,"* Thomas says:

---

[162] Thomas, p. 22.

We need to consider further at this point the question of excluded matters, in relation to what God has required. When God required Noah to build the Ark, he specified that it be made of "gopher" wood. It is easy to see that the stipulation of gopher wood as God's definite will automatically excluded the use of pine or oak or other kinds of wood for the Ark. To have used any wood other than gopher, would have been a deliberate rejection of God's will and a substitution by human authority and therefore sinful.[163]

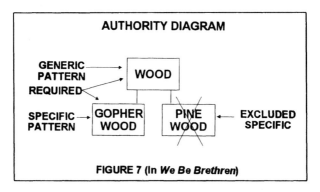

He continues,

Figure 7 vividly portrays the relationship of excluded matters to those that are authorized and required. ... [A]s the diagram shows, other specifics (in this case, pine, oak, etc.) to this same generic (wood) are not only not authorized, but are definitely excluded, ... Note especially that when a specific has been required by God, its generic is authorized as a scriptural requirement, but NO OTHER SPECIFIC to the same generic IS AUTHORIZED. Any other specific would in fact be excluded and sinful. The authorizing or

---

[163] Thomas, p. 24.

requiring of specifics, always authorizes and requires their related generics, but NEVER allows or permits other specifics to the same generics![164]

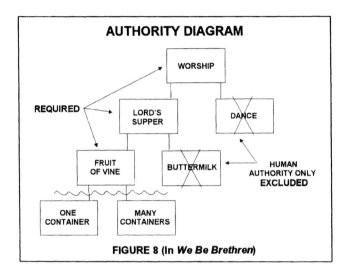

FIGURE 8 (In *We Be Brethren*)

And,

From Figure 8 we can note that when the Fruit of the Vine is required of us and made binding, this fact automatically authorizes and requires its related generics, namely, the Lord's Supper and Worship; since they are both generics in relation to the required item, the Fruit of the Vine. But it is quite obvious that the other specifics that could exist to these same generics, are without Divine authority and they are excluded matters as far as God's will is concerned.[165]

---

[164] Thomas, pp. 24-25.
[165] Thomas, p. 25. I will assume Thomas' expression "Worship" stands for a statement such as "We are to worship God as instructed in the NT."

A required specific excludes any or all additional or substitute actions on its level (or to its generic)![166]

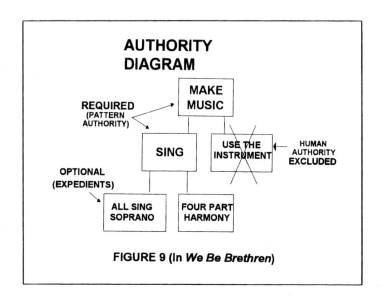

AUTHORITY DIAGRAM

FIGURE 9 (In *We Be Brethren*)

Figure 9 proposes to show how the preceding argument fits the question of Instrumental Music.[167]

---

[166] Thomas, p. 26. By adding *"(or to its generic)"* Thomas is referring to a specific which is on the same level as and under the same generic as the required specific. For example, like "pine wood" is located beside the required "gopher wood" in his Figure 7.

[167] Thomas, p. 26.

Analysis

The essence of what Thomas is saying forms a "T" turned sideways. The upper vertical includes. The downward vertical includes. The horizontal excludes.

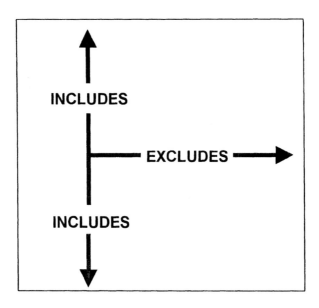

The T is superimposed on generic-specific relationships, to express what can be called two laws of inclusion and one law of exclusion. We can express these laws he is explaining like this: In a hierarchy of generic-specific relationships, where there is a **required** specific,

- that specific authorizes the specifics it includes (the downward vertical),
- that specific authorizes its generic (the upward vertical), and
- that specific excludes (forbids) all other specifics of its generic (the horizontal).

In this discussion, I want to address all three claims, but focus on the horizontal. The whole picture of what Thomas is saying, which includes the T along with the hierarchy, may be illustrated as shown below.

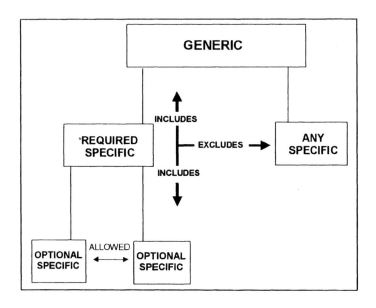

Before discussing each leg of the T, it is important to note that Thomas claims these inclusions and exclusion regarding **required** specifics and not optional specifics. (This is why my illustration shows "allowed" between the optional specifics. And this is why it shows "excludes" only between the required specific and any other specific on its level.) "To specify is to exclude" is ambiguous in that it covers both "to specify as an option is to exclude" and "to specify as a requirement is to exclude." To represent what Thomas is saying without this ambiguity, one needs to understand that the statement "to specify is to exclude" is short for "to specify as a requirement is to exclude."

For example, Thomas' view does not claim that the statement "You **may** use white gopher wood" excludes the statement "You may use dark gopher wood." But his view **is** saying that the statement "You **must** use gopher wood" does exclude (implies the denial of) the statement "You **may** use pine (or any other kind of wood)." So, for the sake of clarity in our quest for truth, when we hear the statement "to specify is to exclude" we could raise a question like, "Do you mean specifying as an option excludes other specifics under the same generic, or do you mean specifying as a requirement excludes other specifics under the same generic?" Mostly, if not always, the "to specify is to exclude" devotee means the latter. Let us now proceed, then, into a study of the three major claims Thomas is making.

The Downward Vertical

A generic does include all of the specifics which make it up. For example, in a diagram, let a block labeled "Worship God" represent all of the NT actions of worship. Such a block implies another block titled "Lord's Supper." Let this block represent all of the NT actions regarding the Lord's Supper. Since the NT **requires** the partaking of the Lord's Supper, then it is a required specific. In turn, the Lord's Supper block implies the block titled Fruit of Vine, which is a required specific under the Lord's Supper block. (Let the block titled "Fruit of Vine" stand for all that the NT instructs regarding drinking fruit of the vine as part of the Lord's supper.) So we have a required generic, under which is a required specific, under which is another required specific. Now we shift to optional specifics.

To fulfill the fruit of the vine requirement, it is not necessary that we drink only **one** specific variety of fruit of the vine, like white grape juice. But it **is** necessary that we drink **some** specific variety of fruit of the vine. Otherwise we would fail to do the God-given requirement of drinking fruit of the vine in the Lord's supper. Since **any** variety of fruit of the vine is fruit of the vine, then, so far, it appears that we have any variety authorized by the required specific "Fruit of Vine." Notice we used the term "necessary" just above, and remember the meaning of implies we showed in our discussion in Part 1 of the book. So now we have several options apparently authorized: the kind of grape from which the juice comes (for example, Concord grape), the color of the juice, its temperature as we are drinking it, the quantity (small cup, half a glass ...), and whatever other possibility. Each of these is an optional specific under the required specific we have labeled Fruit of the Vine. So, apparently, if I drink any of these, then I will have satisfied the action implied by the requirement.

But I must get the whole picture. This is why I said "it appears" and "apparently" above. We have more to do to determine just what is intended in the requirement. One or more of the variations of fruit of the vine might be forbidden elsewhere in the Bible. Using our example, if drinking a variation of the fruit of the vine makes us drunk, then we can know that that variation of drinking the fruit of the vine is excluded.[168] So, all optional specifics under its required generic are okay, except any which the Bible elsewhere denies. And, if the variation under the required generic is not elsewhere denied, then the required generic **itself** authorizes that variation. A generic requirement is, therefore, like an umbrella, authorizing every non-forbidden specific that accomplishes that generic.

---

[168] 1Cor 6:9-10 [9] Do you not know that the unrighteous will not inherit the kingdom of God? Do not be deceived. Neither fornicators, nor idolaters, nor adulterers, nor homosexuals, nor sodomites, [10] nor thieves, nor covetous, nor drunkards, nor revilers, nor extortioners will inherit the kingdom of God.

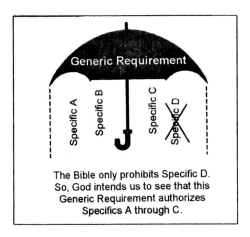

Generic Requirement

Specific A
Specific B
Specific C
Specific D

The Bible only prohibits Specific D.
So, God intends us to see that this
Generic Requirement authorizes
Specifics A through C.

The downward vertical, then, as qualified, represents a true (Biblical) law of inclusion. The authorizing does flow in the downward vertical direction. A statement does include all that its meaning includes. A statement does authorize the teaching and practicing of statements it implies. In so far as Thomas has captured this in his book, he is correct and is to be commended for expressing truth. Let us now go on to his discussion of the upward vertical.

The Upward Vertical

Thomas says,

... when a specific has been required by God, its generic is authorized as a scriptural requirement, ...[169]

The authorizing or requiring of specifics always authorizes and requires their related generics, ...[170]

From Figure 8 we can note that when the Fruit of the Vine is required of us and made binding, this fact automatically authorizes and requires its related generics, namely, the Lord's Supper and Worship; ....[171]

---

[169] Thomas, p. 24.

[170] Thomas, pp. 24-25.

[171] Thomas. p. 25.

There is something wrong here. It is true that NT worship implies the Lord's supper and the Lord's supper implies the fruit of the vine. That is, as just explained, the downward vertical is true. But the Fruit of the Vine block does not imply the Lord's Supper block, and the Lord's Supper block does not imply the Worship block. Thomas is saying too much here. Look back and notice his Figure 8 again (page 203). Notice the terms Lord's Supper and Worship in the boxes. The Lord's Supper is a NT activity which includes more than drinking fruit of the vine. It also includes eating unleavened bread. Worship (assume NT worship) includes all of the Lord's Supper actions plus all the other actions of worship identified in the NT (singing, praying, etc.). So Thomas is explaining and illustrating the upward vertical such that he has a part of the Lord's Supper (the required specific of drinking fruit of the vine) as implying authority for the whole Lord's Supper, and even the whole of worship! If this were true, then we could correctly cite a passage requiring a specific action as proof that we are required to do **all other** actions in its associated generic. For example, the NT passages authorizing drinking fruit of the vine would be proof for authorizing the unleavened bread as well as all NT worship! (One wonders if Thomas wrote what he meant.)

The Worship block and Lord's Supper block in the discussion of the **downward** vertical include all of NT worship and all of the NT instructions about the Lord's Supper, respectively. But when discussing the **upward** vertical we cannot be so inclusive. We can only show the fruit-of-the-vine portion of the Lord's Supper block and only the fruit-of-the-vine-part-of-the-Lord's-Supper portion of the Worship block. The NT worship block implies the whole Lord's Supper block. But the Lord's Supper block does not imply the whole NT worship block.

Now go back to his explanation. Is it true that " ... when a specific has been required by God, its generic is authorized as a scriptural requirement, ..."? No. He is including too much. The requirement to drink fruit of the vine authorizes that part of the Lord's Supper and that part of worship. We certainly can agree with that because a complete thought implies itself. But this is the most we can get out of such a requirement in this upward vertical direction. We will have to find other passages on what else may be required in partaking the Lord's Supper and engaging in worship.

The Horizontal

Let us now begin our analysis of Thomas' claim about the horizontal direction. His law of exclusion claims that requiring a specific in and of itself has the power to exclude (forbid) all other specifics on its same level. Put in other words, he is claiming that a required specific **implies** the denial of its generic's other specifics. He is incorrect. *First*, there is no such **implication** in this direction. It is false, for example, to claim that the statement "We must buy apples" implies (guarantees the truth of the statement) "We must not to buy pears."

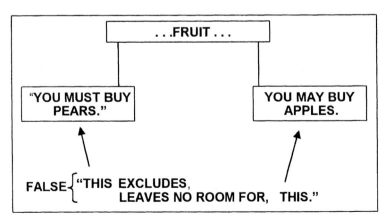

For the above to be true, "You must buy pears" implies "It is not the case that you may buy apples." It would mean that saying "You must buy pears" leaves no room for saying "You may buy apples, " because "to specify is to exclude!" (... pears and ... apples are kinds of the generic "... fruit.") It would mean that once the addressee of the requirement "You must buy pears" hears this, he can **know** just from this statement that he is not to buy apples.

But there is no logical link, no guarantee, that if the first statement is true, the second is true. So, for example, God's specifying to Noah that he make the ark out of gopher wood is not what excluded, forbade, the use of another kind of wood. Rather, what did exclude, forbid, another kind of wood was the fact the God was silent about any other kind of wood. In short, a statement requiring a specific action includes what it includes. But the statement does not exclude (forbid) the specifics which it does not include. (There is one exception to this, which is explained in the next paragraph.) If there is no authority, however, this **does** exclude (forbid). The **conclusion** Thomas expresses is correct: Noah was not to use non-gopher wood. But the reasoning (the "law" of exclusion) he uses to arrive at this conclusion is incorrect. From a false law of exclusion he attempts to draw a conclusion which happens to be true. But the conclusion is true due to a true law of exclusion, namely silence forbids (excludes from righteousness).

A statement includes what it implies. But a statement does not exclude (deny) what it does not imply, with one **exception**. Obviously, any statement denies that which is in logical conflict with it. Take the case where a statement has to do with a must-do action. If a second statement has to do with an action that absolutely prevents doing the first action, then the first does exclude the second. For example, *We are to drink fruit of the* *vine* does imply *We are not to eat unleavened bread during the whole worship service today.* The intended action mentioned in the second statement would consume the whole worship service and thus prevent doing the first action. If a second specific **prevents** doing a required specific, then the required specific does exclude the second. Though I do not always state it, in this book this exception is to be understood. (Note also that a second specific could be forbidden by another passage, independent of the first specific.)[172]

Second, if his law of exclusion were right, then the OT instruction to sing in Ps 68:32[173] would have excluded the OT instruction to use the instrument in Ps 150. Regardless of **why** God granted the use of the instrument in OT worship, the fact is He did. In Ps 150 God required the use of instrumental music in worship and God does not require sin: "Praise" in the

---

[172] Thomas is not **just** saying that a required specific forbids a **substitute** specific. He is saying it forbids any other specific on its level whether that specific is a substitute or an accompaniment: Notice these blanket (unqualified) statements on his pages 24-26: *"The authorizing or requiring of specifics NEVER allows or permits other specifics to the same generics!" "A required specific excludes any or all additional or substitute actions on its level ...!"* Notice these words on his page 29: "As far as our diagram is concerned, the Denominationalist accepts some matters of the box 'ES' type [Excluded Specific, GFB] as being scriptural and proper – for instance, instrumental music in worship. He would say that the command to sing *does not exclude* the use of the instrument. In other words, he feels perfectly free to add to or take from the required matters, in line with his traditions; yet all the while he feels that he is definitely showing allegiance to the Bible. He is not strictly conscious of the need to interpret carefully and exactingly; so, in general, our evaluation of this man is that he is somewhat loose and careless about God's exact requirements and accepts many items of human authority, (Box 'ES' type), without really being aware that he is not being fair to the Bible, to himself, or to God." Thomas, with these words, is telling us the denominationalist is wrong in denying that the sing requirement both forbids adding to (accompaniment) and taking from (substitution).
[173] Ps 68:32 "Sing to God, you kingdoms of the earth; Oh, sing praises to the Lord."

passage is imperative[174] and shows that the use of the instrument in mind is a worship action. If sing in Col 3:16 excludes the use of the instrument as an act of worship in NT times, then sing in Ps 68:32 excluded the use of the instrument as an act of worship in OT times. But wait a minute, Ps 150[175] instructed them to use the instrument in worship. Since God does not conflict with himself, then sing in Ps 68:32 must have left room for (did **not** exclude, forbid) using the instrument as mentioned in Ps 150. Something's wrong, and it is not the Bible: It's this law of exclusion which is wrong: "to specify is to exclude."

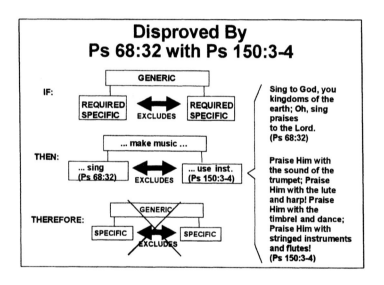

---

[174] Of course, this does not provide authority for us in NT times: Col 2:14-17; Gal 3:24; ....

[175] Ps 150:3-4 "Praise Him with the sound of trumpet; Praise him with the lute and harp! Praise Him with the timbrel and dance; Praise Him with stringed instruments and flutes!"

Third, if this law of exclusion were true, then just one required specific under a generic would exclude all other specifics under that generic. For example, the Lord's Supper, which Thomas lists as a required specific under his generic Worship (his Figure 8), would be sufficient for us to know that all other specifics under worship (such as singing, praying, etc.) are forbidden. So, this law of exclusion forces its adherent to say, if he is consistent, that there could only be one required specific for each generic. This has to be the case because this "law" of exclusion claims that a required specific excludes all other specifics on the same level:

> ... other specifics ... to this same generic ... are not only *not* authorized, but are definitely excluded, and their use would clearly be disobedience to God.[176]
> *The authorizing or requiring of specifics NEVER allows or permits other specifics to the same generics![177]*
> *A required specific excludes any or all additional or substitute actions on its level ...![178]*

---

[176] Thomas, p. 24.

[177] Thomas, pp. 24-25.

[178] Thomas, p. 26. Emphases are by Thomas. We have been focusing on the part of this statement which reads, "A required specific excludes ... all additional ... actions on its level ...." But what about the other part of this statement, having to do with substitution?: "A required specific excludes ... all ... substitute actions on its level ...." This has to do with the one exception we discussed on page 212. The substitution of a required action **is** sin (excluded from righteousness) because then we would not be doing what is **required**. It has nothing to do with specific-to-specific relationships. "On its level" and "specific" in his statement are pinpointing the wrong reason. It is wrong not to do a Biblical must-do even if **no** other action is being done in its place, let alone whether there happens to be a specific-to-specific relationship between the requirement and an action replacing it. Further, a required action implicitly forbids any other action that replaces it. If there is a second action being substituted for a required action, not doing the first is wrong whether that second action itself is righteous or unrighteous. And if that second action is unrighteous, we would be compounding the problem, now committing two sins.

Let's look at some examples. It would be wrong not to fulfill the biblical requirement about singing, even if no action is done in its place. It would be

Fourth, let's think how this law of exclusion would work with the NT plan of salvation. Following Thomas, since the generic for the Lord's supper is Worship, then similarly, using this thinking, the generic for a step in the plan of salvation could be worded like "We are to be saved." (This generic is taught in Acts 2:40 as "Be saved ....") Now, we notice Acts 2:38, which teaches that repentance and baptism are unto salvation. So here we have two specifics under "We are to be saved." The false law of exclusion already results in a problem, because the baptism would exclude the repentance, and the repentance would exclude the baptism. But let's ignore that problem for now, and continue on. The meanings of "We must repent" and "We must be baptized" include all that are included in their meanings. Neither of their literal meanings, however, includes (1) "We must believe in Christ" or (2) "We must jump up and down three times." But this fact (that repent or be baptized does not imply these actions) does not allow a person to use Acts 2:38 as proof that belief and jumping up and down three times are excluded from the plan of salvation. The truth is there is no implication in this horizontal direction which excludes. This is why we know that Acts 2:38 leaves room for the Bible to add other conditions. Of course, we will have to search the rest of the scriptures to find such passages. If one is found teaching belief and/or jumping up and down three times is unto

---

wrong always to substitute Bible reading for it. It would be wrong to replace it with a drunken feast. It would be wrong to replace this act of worship, singing, with dancing or the instrument. But whether or not each of these **second** actions is itself excluded from righteousness has nothing to do with its having some specific-to-specific relationship to the action it is replacing.

A required specific tells us nothing about the righteousness or unrighteousness of the second "specific" "on its level" which is replacing it. Whether the action replacing the required action is itself right or wrong will have to be determined without appealing to the specific-to-specific relationship it might have to that replaced action. It is not the case that an action forbids what it does not include. Of course, if one could think of a second action the doing of which absolutely prevents doing the required action, then he can correctly say that a person cannot do that second action scripturally. But, again, in this case the action would be wrong because it would force one not to do a required action. It would not be wrong due to the fact that it may be a specific on the same level under a common generic.

216

salvation, this would not conflict with Acts 2:38. And if no passage can be found which teaches one or both of these is unto salvation, this also would not conflict with Acts 2:38. This is so because, although a statement implies all which its meaning includes, it **does not** exclude what it does not imply.

We **can** find a passage which teaches that belief in Christ is unto salvation (for example, Rom 10:10[179]). Again, this does not conflict with Acts 2:38, because a statement (Acts 2:38) **does not** exclude what its meaning does not include. So all is well. Now we know that belief, repentance and baptism, all three, are unto salvation.

But we find nothing in the Bible about jumping up and down three times unto salvation. The Bible is silent on this. So what shall we say about this action? Is it included in the plan of salvation or not? Since the all-sufficient Bible teaches us that its absence of an affirmation forbids (Col 3:17; Heb 7:14, and 2 Tim 3:16-17 with 1 Th 5:21; ...), then we know that the silence in the Bible about jumping up and down three times unto salvation forbids such a teaching. So it would be wrong to teach that jumping up and down three times is unto salvation. But we know that this action is denied because (1) the Bible is silent about it and (2) passages inform us that silence forbids. It is not the case that this action is excluded from the plan of salvation by the fact that Acts 2:38 specifies repentance and baptism, for example.

Fifth, if an action has something in common with another action, then we have a class, with specific-to-specific relationships. Now, if the legislator requires one of those specifics, then the required-specific- excludes claim kicks in. Think of how much this excludes. Find any requirement. Find another requirement or option with which the first requirement has something in common. You now have two

---

[179] Rom 10:10 "For with the heart one believes unto righteousness, and with the mouth confession is made unto salvation."

specifics in a genus which conflict with each other – given the required- specifics-excludes (forbids) "rule."[180]

Compare Two Clusters of Principles

There is something emerging from this whole discussion which may be worth our attention at this point. We have been dealing with several principles and these group into two clusters. Let's call these Clusters A and B. Some of us have been teaching one and some the other. These two clusters share principles in common, but differ in one area:

---

[180] Any statement or belief that implies error is false itself and should be abandoned. Thomas himself sees difficulties with the *required specific forbids* belief under the heading "Overlapping Classifications – Some Problems" in *We Be Brethren*. Notice these words from his pages 35-36: "... we have said that **a matter can be an excluded specific to one** pattern requirement, **but** could **also be a** pattern **requirement** itself in another passage. This sounds complicated, but is really rather simple. As an illustration, note that the passage that commands the observance of the Lord's Supper (as a specific to the generic "worship") automatically excludes singing, which is also a specific to the same generic. Singing would from this be sinful in worship, just like instrumental music is, except that in another scripture singing itself is commanded and is established as a pattern requirement! This means that one command, or method of establishing pattern authority, can by the fact of establishing such a pattern, modify the teaching of other pattern matters **which other passages have excluded.**" And on page 37 he says, "*That which is an excluded specific in one relation, and is established as a pattern requirement in another, is a required matter.* (The *pattern requirement* classification is stronger than the *excluded specific* classification and supercedes, when these two overlap in the same point of teaching.)" (Bold are mine, GFB). This is saying that the *required specifics excludes* principle results in contradictory teachings in God's word. Labeling these contradictions with words like "modify" and "supercedes" does not solve the problem. Every principle of Bible interpretation must allow for the truth that all Bible passages are in perfect harmony with one another. Never does God make a statement that conflicts with any other statement He makes. It is true that we need to study other passages that relate to the single passage we are studying. This is to make sure we understand the **intended** meaning the first passage **always had.** But this is not what we have with the principle Thomas is advancing. As expressed by his own words this principle forces a person into saying that one passage actually can exclude (forbid) an action that another requires! Then he uses the misnomers "modify" and "supercedes" for this contradiction he admits is there. Any principle that has a passage conflict with another Bible passage in any way should be abandoned. There is no conflict in **God's** word ever.

Cluster A:
A sentence includes those ideas which its meaning includes. A **sentence does not exclude (forbid) what its meaning does** **not include.** And the silence of the Bible does exclude (forbid).

Cluster B:
*A sentence includes those ideas which its meaning includes. **A*** **sentence excludes (forbids) what it does not include.**[181] And the silence of the Bible does exclude (forbid).

Cluster A is true. This is why Acts 2:38 is consistent with itself (though it has two required specifics steps unto salvation), and why Acts 2:38 and Rom 10:10 are consistent. But Cluster B contains error. So we cannot teach and apply that cluster and be right. If it were true, then Acts 2:38 would conflict with itself because its two specifics would forbid each other. Also, the passage would include all that repentance and baptism include and would **forbid** all specifics unto salvation that these do not include, such as jumping up and down three times unto salvation **and such as belief in Christ unto salvation**. So, if Cluster B were true, Acts 2:38 and Rom 10:10 would be in conflict. The italicized part of the Cluster A includes. The italicized part of Cluster B both includes and forbids. But Cluster B, if true, would forbid so much that the Bible would have many conflicting passages.

The NT requirement *to sing* does not itself forbid the instrument. *Sing* says nothing one way or the other about the use of instrumental music as a means of Christian worship. It leaves room for God to authorize the instrument without logical conflict therefore. It leaves room just like it did in the Old Testament: *sing* in Ps 68:32 and *use the instrument* in Ps 150. Let us notice these Old Testament passages again:

---

[181] Or, *A sentence that expresses a specific requirement excludes (implies the denial of) all other sentences that express specific actions under the same generic.*

219

Sing to God, you kingdoms of the earth; Oh, sing praises to the Lord. (Ps 68:32)

Praise Him with the sound of the trumpet; Praise Him with the lute and harp! Praise Him with the timbrel and dance; Praise Him with stringed instruments and flutes! (Ps 150:3-4)

But, unlike the OT, the NT never does add (authorize) the instrument. Though passages like Col 3:16 leave room for the instrument in Christian worship, the rest of the NT is silent about using it as a means of Christian worship. It is this **silence** which **forbids** the practice today.

The requirement on Noah to use gopher wood did not itself forbid the use of pine. This left room for God to authorize pine. But he never did this. So it is this silence which forbade the practice. Authorizing that priests must be from the tribe of Levi left room for God through Moses to authorize priests being from the tribe of Judah. But he never did this. It was this, the silence, the lack of authority for the practice anywhere in the institution of the priesthood that forbade the practice. This absence of authority was adequate to forbid people from Judah functioning as Old Testament priests, explains the Holy Spirit (Heb 7:13-14 with 8:4-5).

Fifth, the false law of exclusion claims there is not silence where there is. This is so because if "to specify is to exclude" were a true principle, then a required specific under a generic would forbid the other specifics. So, following the reasoning in *We Be Brethren* on this, we could, for examples, cite (a) 1 Cor 11:23-24 (...bread in the Lord's Supper...) to forbid using white chocolate in the Lord's Supper, (b) 1 Pet 3:21 (...baptism...) to forbid jumping up and down three times unto salvation, and (c) Col 3:16 (...singing...) to forbid the instrument in worship. **If we can point to a passage or combination of passages** which explicitly **or implicitly** deals with a particular practice, then the Bible **is not** silent on that practice. This law of exclusion claims these passages implicitly forbid the three actions. But the truth is that in all three of these examples, the Bible is silent. And **since Bible silence forbids**, then these three practices are outlawed. The to-specify-is-to-exclude "law" falsely claims there is no Bible silence where there is!

Objection

Someone says, "But the baptism requirement in Mk 16:15-16 is a generic baptism requirement as to the element in which the immersion is to take place. That is, Mk 16:15-16 says nothing about water. It just requires baptism. Only in other passages do we have water baptism as a specific under this generic (1 Pet 3:20-21, ...). So if we remove the to-specify-is-to-exclude law, we have no basis for excluding non-water baptisms, for they would be authorized by the Mk 16 generic."

Reply

No, No. The baptism must-do in the great commission (Mk 16:15-16; Mt 28:18-20) is **not** a generic requirement as to the element in which to immerse. We can prove from other passages that the intended baptism **IN** this great commission is water baptism. Let us do this now. Notice that, according to the wording of the passage, this baptism is included in the preaching of the Gospel. Now notice that Philip is preaching the Gospel in Acts 8:29-40, and that baptism is identified as water baptism (Act 8:36). So the intended baptism included in the preaching of the Gospel, which is the subject of Mk 16:15-16, is **water** baptism. This we have shown based on the fact that the Holy Spirit always is consistent when discussing the same subject. So we can be sure that passages on the same subject can inform one another.

221

The following facts **also** show that the baptism **built into** Mk 16 is water baptism. Peter is preaching the Gospel in Acts 2 and identifies the purpose of this baptism as forgiveness (Acts 2:38). Now go over to 1 Pet 3:19-21 and notice that the baptism that saves is water baptism. The salvation referenced in this passage is the same as the forgiveness in Acts 2:38, thus showing we have the same baptism. Therefore, the water baptism in 1 Pet 3:20-21 is the same as the baptism in Mk 16:15-16. Therefore, Mk 16:15-16 is **not** generic authority as to the element in which the immersion is to happen. The passage does not authorize both water and non-water immersions. The baptizing in this passage is a required **specific** as to the element of the baptism (water), **not** a required **generic** as to the element.

However, if the Bible had given generic authority on the element of the immersion, then and only then would it have been so inclusive. Then and only then should we accept it so. It is important that we look at the whole Biblical picture on a subject, so as to be sure we have determined the intended level of specificity in a particular passage. (For the record, a person told me once that she asked a minister of a denominational church in Ann Arbor to baptize her in rose pedals. He did it, and as I recall, it was immersion.)

Objection

But isn't the to-specify-is-to-exclude law demonstrated true all the time in daily life? Isn't this the principle followed by the pharmacist when following a doctor's prescription? Isn't the son following this when following his mother's instruction to buy at the store only what she specified? Isn't it this law that justifies the customer's refusal to pay when an auto mechanic changes a muffler when only an oil change was specified?

Reply

Each of these is an instance of silence forbids. The pharmacist does issue those drugs the doctor specified. But he is not to issue drugs about which the doctor's prescriptions are silent. The pharmacist would be doing so without the doctor's authority. The doctor's silence forbids. The son is not to buy candy with the mother's money when she said nothing about candy. Her silence forbids. The auto mechanic is not to change the muffler when the customer was silent about changing the muffler. The customer's silence forbids such action. The forbidding has nothing to do with a specific-to-specific relationship that might exist between the authorized drug and the unauthorized drug, between whatever the mother did authorize and the candy, or between whatever the customer authorized and the muffler. It's the lack of authority that is doing the forbidding in these examples, not whether or not there happens to be a specific-to-specific relationship under the same generic between what was authorized and what was not.

Why the Confusion?

Why are some confused into thinking that required specifics forbid? Why are some saying that it is the directive to *sing* that outlaws the instrument, the directive to *use gopher wood* that interdicts using pine, the directive to *use drug A* that excludes drug B, the directive to *buy yogurt* that denies buying ice cream, the directive to *fix the headlight* that prohibits fixing the muffler? I am not a mind reader, but here are four possibilities.

First, it may be that some folks who see that silence forbids think that this fact depends on or is the same as the required-specifics-excludes principle. They may think that without this principle, we would be opening the box and letting fly many unlawful practices. If this is why some hold to the principle,

223

they need to understand the true Bible silence forbids doctrine and have more confidence in it. God teaches that the silence in His word forbids and He was intentionally silent on certain actions. His word is sufficient for forbidding by silence what He wants forbidden by silence.

A *second* possibility might be found in the distinction between different senses of "exclude." One sense is *not include*. A second is *forbid, deny, interdict, prohibit*. Another way of seeing these two senses is to think about what is being conceived of after the word "from" in "excludes from." That is, excludes from what? The first sense fills this in as "excludes from *the meaning of* or *definition*." The second fills it in as excludes from *righteousness* (because the second sense is *to forbid*.)

Using the first sense, it is true that the **meaning** of a single term or whole sentence excludes other meanings. For example, the meaning of *fish* excludes *telephones*, in the sense it does not include telephones. But the term *fish* tells us nothing about the righteousness or unrighteousness of telephones. Also, the sentence *You must be baptized in water to be saved* excludes that which is not in it, such *as You must jump up and down three times to be saved* or *You must confess belief in Christ to be saved*. However, the first sentence tells us nothing about the righteousness or unrighteousness of the actions expressed in the other two sentences. We would have to go elsewhere to find out about that. *Excludes* here simply means *does not include*.

Thinking in terms of our discussion in this chapter, *excludes* meaning *not include* (*does not imply*) has the downward vertical in mind. The point being made (which is correct) is that a required specific does not authorize actions not under it (that is, actions it does not include). For example,

224

sing does not authorize the instrument and use gopher wood does not authorize use pine. This is all the first meaning of excludes is saying: You do not have authority in the required specific for those actions it does not include. However, the required specific is neutral on whether the actions it does not include are righteous or unrighteous.

The second meaning of excludes, forbids, is used correctly only when Bible-unauthorized actions are in mind. For example, saying God excludes (forbids from righteousness) drunkenness is correct. But sometimes when folks have this second meaning of excludes in mind they are thinking of the horizontal we discussed earlier. The point being made (which is incorrect) is that the required specific forbids (implies the denial of) all other specifics under the same generic.

So then, some may not be rightly dividing the two senses of excludes. If a person starts off his argument with the first meaning, and has the second meaning in mind in his conclusion, he has committed the fallacy of equivocation. This is the fallacy one commits when he confuses in the same argument the different senses a single term has.[182]

Third, some might not be realizing that a requirement implicitly prohibits **any** substitution, due to the fact that it is a requirement. They may not be realizing that this prohibition has no dependence on any specific-to-specific relationship that might exist between the requirement and the substitution. They

---

[182] Like "Since God's saying 'use gopher wood' excludes (does not include) pine, then God excluded (forbade) pine," whereas the sound argument is: "Since God was silent about gopher wood, and His silence excludes (forbids), then God excluded (forbade) pine." For examples, notice how faith-alone adherents equivocate on the words *faith* and *works*. See George F. Beals, "Faith Alone – The Fallacy of Equivocation," *Firm Foundation*, Jan 8, 1985, pp. 1, 4.

might be thinking that the prohibition of a substitution somehow **is** due to a specific-to-specific relationship between the requirement and the substitution. Then, this prohibition also somehow rubs off on added (co-existing) specifics too, thus making up the entire "to specify is to exclude" rule.

Fourth, some might be accepting the to-specify-is-to-exclude claim because they hear respected teachers say it. They may not be thinking it through. The antidote to this is to apply 1 Thes 5:21: "Prove all things; hold fast that which is good." (ASV), and for the respected teacher to do the same. God wants each of us to be an independent thinker. A teacher might be right in one area, and wrong in another.

Summary

This ends my analysis of "What does the forbidding." Let me now summarize what we have been discussing regarding what includes and especially what excludes. *A Biblical statement which requires an action includes all the actions which its meaning includes. The statement thus authorizes these actions, except for any which the Bible elsewhere forbids. The statement does not forbid an action which it does not include, except for any action which denies the requirement. The silence of the Bible does forbid an action. Silence here means there is no passage or combination of passages which has to do with (that is, which requires, permits or forbids) the particular action in question.*

Chapter 23
Closing Remarks

In this final chapter, I offer closing remarks connected with our study, a potpourri, if you will.

- The Restoration Motto
- Infant Baptism an Instance of Bible Silence?
- How Silence and Implication Work Together
- "Farther Than They Perceive the Connection"
- Where Does Instrumental Music Fit In?
- Does God Regulate Worship?
- Summary Passages
- My Privilege

"The Restoration Motto"

A motto is "a sentence, phrase, or word inscribed on something as appropriate to or indicative of its character or use."[183] We find mottoes for countries, companies and other groups, individuals, and movements. In Restoration history, there is a statement attributed to Thomas Campbell that is often called a motto:[184]

---

[183] "motto," *Webster's Third New International Dictionary of the English Language Unabridged*, Philip Babcock Gove, ed. in chief (Springfield, MA: Merriam-Webster Inc., 1986)

[184] For information on the 1809 circumstances that surrounded Thomas Campbell when he expressed the motto, see Earl Irvin West, *Search for the Ancient Order*, Vol. 1 (Nashville, TN: Gospel Advocate Company, 1964), pp. 47-48. West points out that the essence of this motto had been said before in modern times. However, he explains, there was one phase about Campbell's motto that was revolutionary: The Protestants had been applying the principle

227

We speak where the Bible speaks, and are silent where the Bible is silent.

It appears to me that there are several potential uses (functions) bundled into this one statement. Those who say it are not just talking to themselves. So there's an invitation evident: "We are doing a noble thing. Won't you come and join in with us?" There's an exhortation: "Let us all follow the Bible alone." There's a proposal for unity: "Let all who would follow Christ unite and not divide on the basis specified."

Also, the statement has had different meanings to different people over the years. Some of these meanings express Bible truth. Some do not. Here is a meaning G.C. Brewer mentions. He is rebuking those who use the instrument in Christian worship and says,

> They complain that we preach and write and argue against instrumental music in Christian worship, and, in doing this, we are speaking loud, long, and often where the Bible is silent.[185]

> [They] say that in protesting against this practice we are speaking where the Bible is silent.[186]

---

to Roman Catholic traditions. But now some were applying it to Protestant creeds and confessions too. "For the first time there were some who realized that the motto struck with equal force against human creeds as it did against Catholic traditions." p. 47. Let it be noted, however, as we have shown in Part 1, that statements or beliefs which men express are not to be rejected because inference was involved. If they are false, that is why they are to be rejected. The problem is **invalid** reasoning, **unsound** arguments. We **must** use our minds in Bible study. **Proof** is required of us - 1 Th 5:21.

[185] G. C. Brewer, *A Medley on the Music Question* or *A Potpourri of Philology* (Nashville, TN: Gospel Advocate Company, 1948), p. 35.

[186] Brewer, p. 36.

So these folks define the first occurrence of "silent" in the last half of the motto to mean "do not protest." That is, "we do not protest against (do not express denial of) those practices where the Bible is silent." One is reminded of the finger waver who says the modulated "ЈUUUUDGE NOOOOT," misapplying Mt 7:1[187] so that it conflicts with Jn 7:24.[188] There **are** doctrines and behaviors concerning which the Bible is silent against which to protest (to deny), as we show in Part2.

> *We speak where the Bible speaks and*
>
> *are silent where the Bible is silent.*
>
> do not protest

Along the same lines, but expanding, and replacing "Bible" with "Scriptures," James D. North says:

> It is relatively easy to follow the first half of Campbell's famous motto "Where the Scriptures speak, we speak." It is much more difficult to apply the second half: "Where the Scriptures are silent, we are silent." Silence works both ways: Unless there is clear New Testament teaching, we cannot insist that people do certain things; nor can we insist that they

---

[187] Mt 7:1 "Judge not, that you be not judged. 2 "For with what judgment you judge, you will be judged; and with the measure you use, it will be measured back to you."

[188] Jn 7:24 "Do not judge according to appearance, but judge with righteous judgment."

not do certain things. Either way is speaking where
the Bible is silent.[189]

This takes the last half of the motto to mean *we neither
affirm nor deny where the Bible is silent.* This too is not
Scriptural.

```
┌─────────────────────────────────────────┐
│                                          │
│  We speak where the Bible speaks and     │
│                                          │
│  are silent where the Bible is silent.   │
│       ╰────────╮ ╭────────╯              │
│                ╰─╯                        │
│         neither affirm not deny          │
│                                          │
└─────────────────────────────────────────┘
```

There is another possible meaning of the motto I would
like to mention that **the words North uses at least suggest
to my mind.** (See my note in footnote 192.) Notice his
"Unless there is **clear** New Testament teaching." (Emphasis
mine, GFB). This reminds me of verbiage some use in
reference to the explicit-only doctrine. In the next
paragraph, North provides the familiar quote from Thomas
Campbell's *Declaration and Address*:

> Although inferences and deductions from Scripture
> premises, when fairly inferred, may be truly called
> the doctrine of God's holy word, yet are they not
> formally binding....[190]

North then says,
> This idea is dynamite! Campbell is saying: Be sure to
> make a distinction between what Scripture says and
> what you think it means. Logical deductions are

---

[189] James B. North, *Union and Truth: An Interpretive History of the
Restoration Movement* (Cincinnati: Standard Publishing, 1994), p. 90.
[190] North, p. 90.

human conclusions, and they are not to be confused with the teaching of Scripture itself.[191]

Next, he illustrates the point by referring to the Bible-explicit statements "This is my body" (Mt 26:26) and "This is my blood" (Mt 26:28). Then he mentions four teachings about the Lord Supper, including the Roman Catholic doctrine of transubstantiation, for example. Then, he writes:

> But notice that all four of these interpretations are conclusions based on Scripture – none of them are teaching the Scripture in **express** terms. Thomas Campbell would argue that such interpretations are never to be made tests of membership, faith, or fellowship. If Christians today could learn to separate their conclusions based on **Scriptural statements** from the **actual** teaching of **Scripture itself** and never make their own conclusions tests of fellowship, most doctrinal controversies would disappear. (My emphases, GFB)[192]

Putting all of this together (the discussion of the motto, the expression "clear NT teaching," followed next by the quotation on inference from Thomas Campbell, the terms "express," "Scriptural statements," "actual," "Scripture itself") suggests a possible meaning of the motto that distinguishes Bible-explicit from Bible-implicit.

---

[191] North, p. 90.

[192] North, pp. 90-91. We should resist the doctrine of transubstantiation, for example, because it is false: God's Word nowhere affirms it. It results from **incorrect** inference. Heb 9:28 shows it is an implicit prohibition: "... Christ was offered once ...." **Correct** inference is needed, not no inference – 1 Th 5:21. **Note**: I am pleased to point out that in his reply to me dated Aug 7, 1998, North says that he did not and does not believe the interpretation of the motto I explain on page 232.

231

We could express it like this. If by "where the Bible speaks" one means "where the Bible is explicit," and by "where the Bible is silent" one means to include "where the Bible is implicit," then we wind up with something like "We teach where the Bible is explicit, and do not teach where the Bible is implicit." Or, as some would affirm, expressed as an exhortation, "Let us teach (and unite on) where the Bible is explicit, and not divide on where the Bible is implicit." This, of course, is what I have called in our study the *explicit-only doctrine*, which, in Part 1, is shown false (unscriptural).

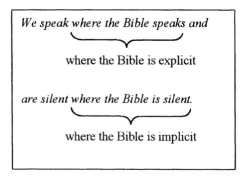

Compare this interpretation of the motto with the words of Dwaine Dunning below:

> For many years, Bible questions have been discussed from the standpoint of a given viewpoint having "command, example and inference" in support. Such use, listing three types of argument without distinction as to value, has given the impression that all three are equal in value. This is not true! And Thomas Campbell, who developed the system, wisely limited it and showed that the third area of "authority," that of inference, was of such a nature that questions affecting

fellowship should never be determined by using inference, or argument by logical process.[193]

Unity comes easily when there is an **explicit** statement of God upon which to base agreement.[194]

Bringing up the rear, miles behind either command or precept, is the third kind of "authority" -- that of inference. This kind of "authority" rests almost wholly on human wisdom.[195]

There can never be unity in human inference.[196]

Calvinism and Arminianism, the perseverance of the saints, instruments of music and four-part harmony, owning a church building, painting "holy pictures" or destroying them, immersing in river or baptismal tank, questions regarding the millennium these are just a few of the divisive subjects which in no way depend on divine command or apostolic precedent, but which come entirely within the third realm, that of inference, and are upheld and opposed in such a way that the unity which God commanded is destroyed for the sake of being right or wrong about something that has only imperfect reasoning to affirm or deny! This is, with a vengeance, "leaving the commandment of God that you may establish your own traditions."[197]

[193] Dwaine Dunning, "The Authority of Inference," *Mission Messenger*, Sept 1970, p. 132. One wonders what kind of argument there is but by "logical process." Wrangling (emotionalism)?
[194] Dunning, p. 133. (My emphasis, GFB.)
[195] Dunning, p. 133.
[196] Dunning, p. 133.
[197] Dunning, p. 134.

As we have already pointed out, even Bible-explicit statements involve implication. Further, much of Dunning's insistence above about the non-Bible explicit is non-Bible explicit. See Part 1 and Chapter 18 for adequate replies.

Next, G.C. Brewer provides the following meaning of the motto, resulting in the refreshing words I have placed in bold letters:

> the meaning of this well known motto is that **we practice that which the Bible authorizes and we decline to practice that which the Bible does not authorize.**[198]

He continues,

> To *remain silent* means that we will *stop practicing* where the Bible *stops teaching*.; that our practice in matters of religion is limited by the word of the Lord, restricted by divine revelation.[199]

This understands "speak" in the motto to mean *practice*, "speaks" to mean *authorizes*, the first occurrence of "silent" to mean *decline to practice* (that is, *not practice*), and the second meaning of "silent" to mean *not authorize*. To arrive here from the motto, one is assigning two different meanings to speak(s) in the "We speak where the Bible speaks" half of the motto, and two different meanings of "silent" in the "be silent where the Bible is silent" half. This happens in rhetoric, though the two switches in mid-stream may be confusing at first. Also, this meaning of the motto

---

[198] Brewer, p. 35. (My emphasis, GFB.)
[199] Brewer, p. 35.

equates the more narrow *Bible silence* with the wider *Bible unauthorized.* (See my *How Unauthorized and Silence Differ* in Chapter 11.) Notice that one could go right to Brewer's fine statement from the Scriptures (Col 3:17), rather than through the motto.

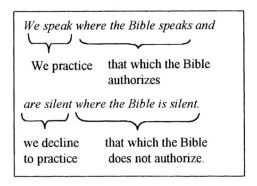

One sister said that she thinks many people express the motto as another way of saying the wonderful: "Do not add to or take away from the Bible." I suspect this is true.

Some provide an abbreviated summary of the motto's different interpretations as Bible silence forbids versus Bible silence permits.

There are at least four possible challenges one might face when trying to arrive at an overall statement from the motto: (1) Assigning a meaning to **the individual words** Campbell chose (*speaks, silent, ...*) so that together they express the overall statement claimed. (2) Trying to find **one** meaning for **both** occurrences of *speak,* and **one** meaning for **both** occurrences of *silent* in Campbell's statement. After trying this, you may decide to use different meanings as Brewer did above. (3) Defining just who and who are not included in the "we" and whether the declarative statement is true of that "we." (Note that this goes away if you replace the "we" with "let us," changing the declarative to an exhortation.). And (4) whether you want to try to determine and then retain Thomas Campbell's original intent, or just take the meaning according to the words themselves, without the background.

An interesting exercise is to ask individuals or a Bible class to fill out the form below, then compile and compare the results, in light of the Scriptures. Expect variety.

How do you understand the motto?

Let us speak	where the Bible speaks	and be silent	where the Bible is silent.
This part means:	This part means:	This part means:	This part means:

So the whole statement means:

A brother in an adult Bible class thought the motto is unclear. So he suggested replacing it with a clearer statement like, *Everything we do, we do only with Bible authority.* "Then we are simply expressing the truth taught in Col 3:17!," he said! We can do that and be right with God. Note, though, that it is unnecessary to abandon any such statement so long as it is taught by His Word.

236

Here are suggested guidelines for inscribing a statement on His Cause "as appropriate to or indicative of Its character:"

1. Don't place yourself in a situation where, if someone asks you, "What does that mean?", you have to think to yourself, "Hmm. I need to check with someone else to find out what I mean!" Be an independent thinker, as instructed in 1 Th 5:21A. ("Test all things;").

2. Do not use or endorse any statement of such import as we are discussing, unless and until you yourself see that it is Biblical – 1 Th 5:21B. ("hold fast what is good.").

3. As much as it depends on you, make sure the meaning of a statement of such import is clear to your audience – Jas 3:5. ("... the tongue is a little member and boasts great things. See how great a forest a little fire kindles!")

We now turn to another topic of interest.

Is Infant Baptism an Instance of Bible Silence?

Some through the years have referred to infant baptism as an example of where the Bible is silent. Is it? Another way of asking the question is: Is there a Bible passage or combination of Bible passages to which you can point that explicitly or implicitly requires, permits or forbids the infant baptism doctrine? If the answer is Yes, then the Bible is not silent on the practice. As expected, members of the adult Bible class in the Saline (MI) church of Christ cited several **existing** passages that refute the doctrine of infant baptism, thereby showing that it is not an instance of Bible silence. Among the lines of reasoning we discussed were these arguments. Some of these overlap:

1. The (only) Bible plan for saving alien sinners itself refutes the doctrine: There are prerequisites to Bible baptism (Rom 10:17; Acts 2:38; Rev 22:17; ...)[200] which infants cannot do. This fact, coupled with God's attributes of love, omniscience and fairness, refute it, because God would not require an infant to follow the impossible.
2. The meaning of *baptizo* refutes that formulation of infant baptism that allows sprinkling or pouring to replace Bible baptism. I observed: Any practice that replaces a Biblical requirement is disproved by that requirement implicitly.
3. The doctrine incorrectly attributes inherited sin to infants. Ezk 18:20.[201]

So we concluded that the Bible contains at least one passage that implicitly prohibits the doctrine. So there is something there in the Bible dealing with the subject, and thus not nothing, not silence. Infant baptism **is** an example of a Bible-unauthorized action, since all Bible-addressed prohibitions are Bible-unauthorized actions. But it is not an example of a Bible-silent action.

Silence and Implication Work Together

Silence and implication, though different, work together. Here is how:

*   (A) The Bible forbids all actions about which it is silent. (2 Tim 3:16-17 with 1 Thes 5:21; etc.)
*   (B) The Bible is **silent** about action x.
*   (C) Therefore, the Bible forbids action x.

---

[200] Rom 10:17 "So then faith *comes* by hearing, and hearing by the word of God." Acts 2:38 "Repent, and let every one of you be baptized in the name of Jesus Christ for the remission of sins; and you shall receive the gift of the Holy Spirit." Rev 22:17 "...Whoever desires, let him take the water of life freely."

[201] Ezk 18:20 "The soul who sins shall die. The son shall not bear the guilt of the father, nor the father bear the guilt of the son. The righteousness of the righteous shall be upon himself, and the wickedness of the wicked shall be upon himself."

Only statement B is making a silence claim. B constitutes part of the evidence that leads to the conclusion C. A and B **combine** to **imply** C. That is, it is impossible for A and B to be true, and for C to be false.

"Farther Than They Perceive the Connection"

Thomas Campbell says deductions are not to be bound farther than people see the connection. (See quotations on pages 30-31.). As we show below, there is to be room for growth in Christ. Yet, note these observations about Campbell's statement: (1) If a person affirms that implicit Bible truths are not to be bound farther than people see the connection, then will he affirm that implicit Bible truths **are** to be bound when people **do** see the connection? If so, he admits some are to be bound. Yet, this itself conflicts with the wide-sweeping claims some people have and are making about inferential truths. (2) People do not comprehend explicit Bible truths too. Ignorance is not limited to implicit Bible truths. So will the explicit-only devotees affirm we are not to bind explicit Bible truths of which people are ignorant? To be consistent they should. Why the focus just on the implied then? Indeed, it is true that **in Christ** there is to be growth (2 Pet 3:18; Phil 3:16).[202] But, as we have pointed out, this is not limited to implicit Bible truths. There is also growth in learning explicit Bible truths. Whatever we conclude about such implicit truths must also be concluded about such explicit truths. (3) Is

---

[202] 2 Pet 3:18 "but grow in the grace and knowledge of our Lord and Savior Jesus Christ." Phil 3:14-16 "[14] I press toward the goal for the prize of the upward call of God in Christ Jesus. [15] Therefore let us, as many as are mature, have this mind; and if in anything you think otherwise, God will reveal even this to you. [16] Nevertheless, to *the degree* that we have already attained, let us walk by the same rule, let us be of the same mind."

ignorance of seeing the connection all that Thomas Campbell and modern writers who appeal to his statement are saying? No. They more widely dismiss inferential truths as binding. See quotations from Thomas Campbell (pp. 30-31), Alexander Campbell (p. 32), and the many quotes provided throughout Part 1. Of course, none is consistent with such a claim.

Where Does Instrumental Music Fit In?

The use of instrumental music in worship used to be of more concern to professed Christians than it has been to many in more recent times. Notice this nineteenth century statement:

Sanction of instrumental music in worship is supposed by many to be found in Eph. v. 10 and Col. iii. 16, where occurs the word ψάλλω, which, it is alleged, means to sing with the accompaniment of a harp. But this argument would prove that it is as much a duty to play as to sing in worship. It is questionable whether, as used in the New Testament, ψάλλω means more than to sing. But, even admitting that it retains an instrumental allusion, we may hold, with Meyer and others, that it does so only figuratively; the heart being the seat or the instrument of the action indicated. The absence of instrumental music from the worship of the church for some centuries after the apostles, and the sentiment regarding it which pervades the writings of the Fathers, are unaccountable, if in the apostolic church such music was used.[203]

---

[203] "Psalms," *A Religious Encyclopaedia or Dictionary of Biblical, Historical, Doctrinal, and Practical Theology, Based on the Real-Encyclopadie of Herzog, Plitt and Hauck.* Philip Schaff, ed. (New York: Funk & Wagnalls Company, 1881), III, p. 1961. The spine of this publication reads "Schaff-Herzog Encyclopedia of Religious Knowledge, Volume III. Mabillon-Ryland." This article ("Psalms") was authored by James Harper. He provides titles of pro-instrument and anti-instrument publications. His words exactly are: "In Favor of Instrumental Music. Alexander Fleming: *Letters and Answers*, 1808;

Overlapping Harper's thought that is expressed in the last sentence of the foregoing quotation are these from more recent times:

The development of Western music was decisively influenced by the exclusion of musical instruments from the early Christian Church.[204]

In the beginning, all the Christian musical practices were vocal, ...[205]

... for virtually the first thousand years of its history Church music was destined to be unaccompanied.[206]

Anonymous: *Organs and Presbyterians*, Edinburgh, 1829; D. F. Bonner: *Instrumental Music divinely authorized in the Worship of God*, Rochester, N.Y. 1881. Against Instrumental Music. John Calvin: *Commentary on Psalm cl.*; Gisbertus Voetius: *Politicae Eccl.*, vol. I. Lib. 2, tract. 2 cap. 2, Amsterdam, 1663; James Begg: *The Use of Organs in Christian Worship Indefensible*, Glasgow, 1886; James Glasgow: *Heart and Voice*, Belfast, 1874 (?); D. W. Collins: *Musical Instruments in Divine Worship condemned by the Word of God*, Pittsburgh, Penn., 1881; James Harper: *A Counterblast to the Organ*, New York, 1881." I did not see these words I have quoted from Harper under "Psalms" in *The New Schaff-Herzog Encyclopedia of Religious Knowledge*, Samuel Macauley Jackson, ed.-in-chief (Grand Rapids: Baker Book House, 1964). The latter work has more volumes than the older version. Its front matter says "Exclusive American publications rights secured by Baker Book House from Funk and Wagnalls." Its first printing is dated July, 1950. Apparently, not only has the instrument in worship "won the day" with many (but not all). Even interest in the history of the controversy has waned with many. Being unaware of the argumentation can result in shortsightedness: Thinking that what's in vogue in our own day is the way it has always been all the way back to New Testament times. In other words, folks could fall into the trap of defining the past (even Bible teaching) solely in terms of their own time and place! What not to include in a publication, though, is a judgment call, albeit perhaps unwise.

[204] Paul Henry Lang, *Music in Western Civilization* (New York: W.W. Norton & Company, Inc., 1941), p. 54.
[205] Howard D. McKinney and W. R. Anderson, *Music in History: The Evolution of an Art* (New York: American Book Co., 1957), p. 80.
[206] Alan Kendall, *Music Its Story in the West* (New York: Arco Publishing, Inc., 1980), p. 11.

And, notice these excerpts from an English publication dated 1698[207] whose title page I show below. The author is concerned about the introduction of an organ in a parish church of the Church of England. You will notice that at times he provides refutations of "Mr. Newte's" quotations of "Mr. Baxter."

A

LETTER

TO A

Friend in the Country,

Concerning the Use of

INSTRUMENTAL MUSICK

IN THE

𝕎𝕠𝕣𝕤𝕙𝕚𝕡 𝕠𝕗 𝔾𝕠𝕕:

IN

Anſwer to Mr. *Newte's* SERMON Preach'd at *Tiverton* in *Devon*, on the Occaſion of an Organ being Erected in that Pariſh-Church.

LONDON:

Printed for *A. Baldwin*, at the *Oxford-Arms* in *Warwick Lane*. 1698.

---

[207] *A Letter to a Friend in the Country, concerning the Use of Instrumental Music in Worship...* (London: Printed for A. Baldwin, at the Oxford-Arms in Warwick Lane, 1698). The quotations I provide are photocopies of the book on microfilm: Ann Arbor: University Microfilms International, n. d., Film X440, Reel 1209:13.

From page 5:

> I perceive that Mr. Newte was enforced to have recourse to the Old Testament for a Text, that his Sermon might keep Tune with his Organ. He was well aware that the New-Testament would not afford him one, to answer his Design.

I perceive that Mr. Newte was enforced to have recourse to the Old Testament for a text, that his sermon might keep tune with his organ. He was well aware that the New Testament would not afford him one, to answer his design.

From page 17:

> But he enquires, *Why both should not be abolished, or neither?* Methinks the reason is plain. Because the continuation of the one is expressly enjoined in the New Testament, as *Ephes.* 5. 19. and *Col.* 3. 16. But there is *Nothing* in the whole New Testament to warrant, or Encourage the Use of *Instrumental Musick.*

But he enquires, Why both should not be abolished, or neither? Methinks the reason is plain. Because the continuation of the one is expressly enjoined in the New Testament, as Ephes 5:19 and Col 3:16. But there is nothing in the whole New Testament to warrant, or encourage the use of instrumental music.

From page 46:

> Mr. Baxter's Fourth Argument is this. *No Scripture forbiddeth it, therefore it is not unlawful.* This Argument as made use of by some Men, has frequently been encountred and foiled. (1.) If he means that no Scripture does *expresly* forbid it, and from thence concludes it Lawful; then will it follow, that what ever things the Scripture does not *expresly* forbid may lawfully be used in the Worship of God. Which allowed will be a very fair plea for a Multitude of *Popish* Ceremonies. Then Holy-water, Crucifixes, Altars, Oyl, Salt and Cream in Baptism may be harmlesly used. For the Sacred Scriptures do not any where *expresly* caution against them. Upon this pretence, how many things might be introduced into the Christian Worship?

Mr. Baxter's fourth argument is this. No scripture forbiddeth it, therefore it is not unlawful. This argument as made use of by some men, has frequently been encountered and foiled. (1) If he means that no scripture does expressly forbid it, and from thence concludes it lawful; then will it follow that what ever things the scripture does not expressly forbid may lawfully be used in the worship of God. Which allowed will be a very fair plea for a multitude of popish ceremonies. Then holy water, crucifixes, altars, oyl, salt and cream in baptism may be harmlessly used. For the sacred scriptures do not any where expressly caution against them. Upon this pretence, how many things might be introduced into the christian worship?

Now that you have practiced with the foregoing old English, lastly, I provide these words from page 47. However, I do so without the modern accompaniment and with apologies for the appearance. The writer of this seventeenth-century text sees that a generic requirement authorizes specifics that implement it: what I have called in Chapter 22 "the downward vertical."

Mr. *Baxter's* Fifth Argument is to this purpose. *Nothing can be said against it* (Inftrumental Mufick) *that I know of, but what is faid against Tunes, and Melody of Voice.* I Anfwer, (1.) I humbly conceive that a great deal more may be faid againft it. For thus much is certain, that God has enjoyned us Vocal Singing, and commanded us to make Melody in the Praifing of him. Now Sing we cannot, but we muft make ufe of fome Tune or other ; Some fort of Melody or other, muft be made for the difcharging this Duty. Now feeing God has left us no Direction in what Tune he would have us Sing, it is moft apparent, that he has left us at liberty as to this Matter. Seeing he has made vocal Singing our Duty by a plain command ; he has thereby made *Tune* disjunctively neceffary. Not that this, or that, *Singly* confidered, is neceffary ; but fome *Tune* or other *disjunctively*: And fo God has left it to Chriftians themfelves to determine of the particular *Tunes* they will praife God by. But God has not any way Commanded Inftrumental Mufick ; it cannot be reduced to any precept of the Gofpel either *directly* or *disjunctively*. True it is, If God had been pleafed to have commanded us the Celebrating his Praifes with Mufical Inftruments ; without fpecifying what fort he would have imployed in that cafe; then Perfons would not have been obliged to any particular fort of them ; but they might have ufed either Pfalteries, or Harps, or Viols, or Organs, as they fhould have found to have been moft Convenient for that purpofe. But alas! God has not enjoyned us the ufe of Inftrumental Mufick at all in Religious Duties, and therefore there is no realon Perfons fhould be follicitous about the fort of them. Well then, *Tune* being *disjunctively* confidered, falling under a Divine Command, and Mufical Inftruments however confidered falling under none, I fuppofe a Man may fay, that more may be faid for *Tunes*, than for Inftrumental Mufick in the Worfhip of God under the Gofpel. (2.) I believe we may be able to fay *a little more* againft Inftrumental Mufick in the Worfhip of God, than can be faid againft *Tunes*, and *Melody* in Vocal Mufick. When we fhall come to confider Mr. *Newts* Anfwers to Objections, I fuppofe you may be convinced of this ; therefore, thither I refer you.

244

So then, where does God's word categorize the use of instrumental music as to obligations and options? Many today would locate all of its use under the option block in the figure below.

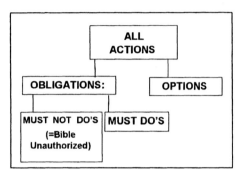

Actually, we need to divide the question, for there are two uses to consider: **worship** and **non-worship**. This bifurcation is necessary due to the setting off of worship from other activities by Jn 4:24, "… must worship Him in spirit and truth." (For more on this setting off, see item 60 in *Topics for Study and Discussion* at the end of the book.) One non-worship use of the instrument is to make a living, for example. First Tim 5:8 authorizes this use. Here is how: The passage gives generic authority for providing for one's own. And, no NT passage forbids using the instrument for this, as long as the instrument is not used as a means of worship. So 1 Tim 5:8 locates such use under the options category in our figure.

But due to the added restriction of Jn 4:24 regarding worship activity, we must now find authority for using the instrument **in worship**. Further, notice that Jn 4:24 is not qualified as to where the worship is done. So we must find Bible authority for all worship of God (including the singing of spiritual songs), wherever it is done: in the assembly, at home alone, etc. So where does instrumental music as an act of

245

worship fit in? Frankly, I struggled with this question, having come out of the Episcopal Church with its organ, choir, ... But I decided to remove my feelings and base my conclusions solely upon finding Bible authority for my actions. I have yet to find proof that instrumental music in **worship** is authorized and thus locate it along side using a third element for the Lord's supper, as pictured below. In his chapter of the book, *The Instrumental Music Issue,* Jack P. Lewis says it like this: "The survey of the New Testament which we have completed has shown that music was a part of the worship of the New Testament, but it has also shown that the New Testament is completely silent about the use of instrumental music in worship."[208] Note this reasoning: Since (1) *instrumental music in worship is an instance of Bible silence* and (2) *Bible silence is a subset of Bible-unauthorized actions,* and (3) *the Scriptures locate all Bible-unauthorized actions as Must Not Do's,* then (Conclusion) *the Scriptures locate instrumental music in worship as a Must Not Do.* The only way to show that instrumental music in worship is not in this category is to **prove** that God authorizes it for today. God's will is not determined by what is or is not popular in church history.[209]

---

[208] Everett Ferguson, Jack P. Lewis, Earl West, *The Instrumental Music Issue,* Bill Flatt, ed. (Nashville: Gospel Advocate Company, 1987), p. 47.

[209] For more discussion along these lines see James D. Bales, *Instrumental Music and New Testament Worship* (Searcy, Arkansas: Resource Publications, 1973); Everett Ferguson, *A Capella Music in the Public Worship of the Church* (Abilene, Texas: Biblical Research Press, 1972). For a concise and persuasive analysis see Thomas B. Warren's article, "Liberalism and the Use of Instrumental Music in the Worship of God" in *The Church Faces Liberalism: Being the Freed-Hardeman Lectures of 1970, Henderson, Tennessee* (Nashville: Gospel Advocate Company, 1970), pp. 243-256. At the writing of this footnote, there was a long compilation of quotations on instrumental music in worship from encyclopedias, dictionaries and other sources at the following internet web site: http://www.bible.ca/H-music.htm. Note that web sites change. Similar lists may be found in M. C. Kurfees, *Instrumental Music in Worship* (1911; rpt. Nashville: Gospel Advocate Company, 1969), and in two articles by F. W. Gould: "The Instrumental Music Question" and "Encyclopedias and Histories Testify" in two consecutive issues of *The Word of*

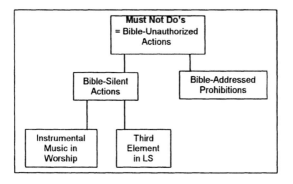

Does God Regulate Worship?

In his 1881 publication on instrumental music in worship, James Harper, a Presbyterian, raised and replied to this important question: "What is the fundamental principle or law for the regulation of worship?" This question has to do with any act of worship. At the time he wrote, he claimed there were at least these four distinguishable views on this among professed Christians:

> I. The Romish. This is to the effect that the Church, which now means virtually the Pope, has authority to prescribe modes of worship, subject only to this limitation, that none be enjoined which is forbidden in either the Scriptures, or the patristic traditions in the custody of the Church. Forms and ceremonies decreed in this spirit are held to be binding upon the conscience.

Life, Franklin Camp, ed. (Birmingham, Alabama: Shades Mountain Church of Christ), May, 1974, pp. 1-3, and June 1974, pp. 1-2.

II. The Anglican. The tenor of this view, is that the Church, guided by the general principle, "Let all things be done decently and in order," may decree rites and ceremonies additional, though not contrary to the express or plainly implied enactments of Scripture, and that forms so decreed are authoritative over the conscience. The only appreciable difference between this and the Romish view, is that this recognizes the Scriptures alone as the limiting standard, whereas by the Romanist, the traditions of the Church are put on a level with the Scriptures, as a standard of faith and practice; while, besides, he regards certain apocryphal writings as included in the Scriptures.

III. The Lutheran, or Compromise view. The substance of this view is that the Church may adopt certain rites and forms of worship which have not been appointed in the word of God, provided that no one who is conscientiously opposed to them shall be forced to compliance, or be subjected to censure for his non-conformity. This position was taken by some of the earlier Puritans in England, who were not disposed to protest seriously against some ornamental additions to the Scriptural forms of worship, but were averse to compulsion in the matter, and disinclined to say that they felt bound in conscience to compliance. In coarse of time the Puritans reached clearer views and firmer footing; the doctrine about to be announced having gained acceptance with them.

IV. The Westminster or Radical view. The essence of this doctrine is that no form of worship is admissible without divine appointment, and that every form so appointed, is carefully to be observed according to prescription.

Harper continues,

I have called this the "Westminster" view, because it is the law of worship recognized expressly in the formularies drawn up by the famous "Assembly of Divines" convened at Westminster Abbey, London, in the seventeenth century.

The doctrine in question, however, was not broached first by that Assembly. It was the doctrine of Calvin, of most of the Reformed Churches of the Continent, and of the Church of Scotland, and had been acted upon by them before the sitting of the Westminster Assembly.

That the Westminster Confession and Catechisms teach the view just stated needs, perhaps, to be proved, inasmuch as many who profess adherence to them, and are recognized as authoritative expounders of them, appear to write and act as if no such principle had been annunciated in those documents. Some attention, will, therefore, be bestowed upon this point.

In Chapter I, Section 6, of the Confession of Faith, occur these words: - "The whole counsel of God, concerning all things necessary for his own glory and man's salvation, faith and life, is either expressly set down in Scripture, or by good and necessary consequence may be deduced from Scripture; unto which nothing at any time is to be added, whether by new revelations of the spirit or traditions of men."[210]

---

[210] James Harper, *A Counterblast to the Organ; or, The Lawfulness of Using Instrumental Music in Worship During the Present Dispensation Discussed and Denied* (New York: Magill & De La Mare, 1881), pp. 8-9. Notice Harper's use of "Radical" describing what he calls the "Westminster" view.

From our study in this book, we can see the Biblical reply to Harper's question, "What is the fundamental principle or law for the regulation of worship?" The Bible teaches this answer: *Whatever action you do, including any worship action, do only if there is divine authority for it.* And, modifying what Harper says, I would express his 1881 claims like this, with some addition:

1. **One View on Divine Silence.** The silence in Scripture, in the apocryphal writings and in Church Tradition regarding an act of Christian worship **permits** the church authorities to decide whether or not the members will practice that act of worship.

2. **A Second View on Divine Silence.** The silence in Scripture regarding an act of Christian worship **permits** church authorities to decide whether or not the members will practice that act of worship.

3. **A Third View on Divine Silence.** The silence in Scripture regarding an act of worship **permits** church authorities to decide whether or not the members will practice that act of worship, except when a member cannot conscientiously engage in the action. In this case, the member is excused from participating.

4. **A Fourth View on Divine Silence.** The silence in Scripture regarding **some** actions (namely, "religious" actions), **forbids** those actions.

5. **The Scriptural View on Divine Silence.** The silence in Scripture regarding **any** action **forbids** that action. (2 Tim 3:16-17 with 1 Thes 5:21; Col 3:17; Heb 1:4-5; etc. Notice the "every" in 2 Tim 3:17 and "whatsoever," "in word or in deed," and "all" in Col 3:17.) Therefore, the silence in Scripture regarding an act of **worship** forbids that action.

This English word derives from the Latin *radix*, meaning *root*. "Radical" is defined as "1. of or proceeding from the root. 2. of or proceeding from the root or origin: original, fundamental. 3. marked by a considerable departure from the usual or traditional; extreme, drastic, thoroughgoing." *Webster's Third New International Dictionary Unabridged*, ed. in chief Philip Babcock Gove (Springfield, MA, 1986). Harper hardly means definition 3. He is saying that what he calls the "Westminster" view is the original (that is, Scriptural) view.

Summary Passages

Here are passages that sum up the study we have made in this book. From these passages, we can form wonderful exhortations to ponder and apply throughout our lives:

[21]Test all things; hold fast what is good. [22]Abstain from every form of evil. (I Th 5:21-22)

[17]And whatever you do in word or deed, *do* all in the name of the Lord Jesus, giving thanks to God the Father through Him. (Col 3:17)

[15]Be diligent to present yourself approved to God, a worker who does not need to be ashamed, rightly dividing the word of truth. (2 Tim 2:15)

My Privilege

It has been a privilege to have made this journey in His world of ideas and to have discovered for myself these jewels of truth: how Bible implication binds and Bible silence forbids. I would like to say this to those individuals whose mistaken views deny implication or Bible silence forbids: I carry no animosity, dear reader. It is my prayer, rather, that we recognize the vital role He wants both His implicit teachings and His silence to have in people's lives. May each of us, as necessary, change our views to match His, and thus contribute to, rather than resist, His Cause.

I give all this exhortation first: Assure that your soul prospers. Then, may 3 Jn 2 be yours.

For Study and Discussion

PART 1: IMPLICATION
1. Define implication.
2. Give an example of implication.
3. Give an example of no implication.
4. Explain what an explicit Bible teaching is.
5. Give an example of an explicit Bible teaching.
6. Explain what an implicit Bible teaching is.
7. Give an example of an implicit Bible teaching.
8. Can you identify a Bible teaching which the Bible teaches neither explicitly nor implicitly?
9. What is the explicit-only doctrine?
10. Refute the explicit-only doctrine.
11. Are you sure that the Bible teaches *God so loved you that He gave His only begotten Son*?
12. Are the italicized words in 11 an explicit Bible teaching or an implicit Bible teaching?
13. Express the argument form which concludes *X is true*, where X is any doctrine which the Bible teaches.
14. Compare the statement *God is not going to allow us to bind on others conclusions we have arrived at by inference and deduction* with 1 Thes 5:21. Are the two statements in harmony? Explain.
15. Is the *if, then* structure of the following statement in harmony with the claim being made by the double-underlined part of the statement? Explain.

> If <u>God did not allow the Jewish Christians at that time to bind on others things He Himself had commanded,</u> <u>God is not going to allow us to bind on others conclusions we have arrived at by inference and deduction.</u>

16. Are Aristotle's logic and syllogisms in conflict with the Lord?

17. Did Thomas and Alexander Campbell teach the explicit-only doctrine at least in some of their writings?
18. Does the fact that we should follow the Bible disallow affirming and perpetuating some statements human beings have made? Explain.
19. Summarize what each of the writers quoted in Chapters 7 through 9 say about the use of logic in Bible study.
20. Compare the summaries in item 19 above with the following passages: Is 1:18; 1 Pet 3:15; 1 Thes 5:21. Are they in harmony with these passages, or in conflict? Explain.

PART 2: SILENCE FORBIDS
21. Chapter 10 refers to two distinctions: (1) explicit versus non-explicit and (2) implicit versus nothing. Explain and illustrate the two.
22. Explain how silence and implication differ.
23. Explain why a person sets himself up for difficulty if by silence he includes implication.
24. Give a precise definition of Bible silence.
25. Explain how unauthorized and silence differ in meaning.
26. Identify and illustrate the possible ways of interpreting silence. Can you think of additional illustrations of silence permits and silence forbids from daily life?
27. Give an example of an action about which the Bible is silent.
28. Does Bible silence leave us in the dark? Explain.
29. If it were the case that Bible silence on an action leaves us in the dark, would Rom 14:23 give us instruction on whether or not we should do that action? Explain.
30. Explain how *Bible silence forbids* and *Bible silence permits* differ in meaning.
31. Explain the Bible silence forbids argument which is based on 2 Tim 3:16-17 with 1 Thes 5:21; and explain the two objections and replies regarding 2 Tim 3:15-17 found in Chapter 15.
32. Explain the Bible silence forbids argument which is based on Col 3:17.

33. Explain the Bible silence forbids argument which is based on Heb 7:13-14 with 8:4-5; and explain the objection and reply to this argument found in Chapter 17.

34. For the sake of seeing the point, let us assume the *to specify is to exclude* "law" is true. Now, with this view, respond to the following two items: (a) Explain how Ex 27:21-28:4 implicitly prohibits anyone from Judah from functioning as a priest. (b) Explain how the nothing in Heb 7:14 leaves room for the something (the implicit prohibition according to this view) in Ex 27:21-28:4.

35. Can you prove that Heb 7:13-14 with 8:4-5 teaches that Bible silence forbids is both a NT doctrine and an OT doctrine? Explain.

36. Is the doctrine of Heb 1:4-5 that no angel is king an instance of Bible silence? Does Heb 1:4-5 affirm that Bible silence forbids is both an OT and a NT doctrine? Explain your answers.

37. Read the Modern Things Forbidden? and Paralyzed into Non-action? sections of Chapter 19. Read item 55 below. Does the inclusive language in 2 Tim 3:16-17, 1 Thes 5:21 and Col 3:17 show that we must have Biblical authority for only **some** human actions (such as only worship actions, religious actions, or the like) or for **all** human actions? If one answers "only some," then which of our actions are and which are not included? What criteria do we use to tell that this action requires Biblical support, but that does not? Or, are there terms in the passages which show that **all** our actions must have Biblical authorization? And if you answer "all," then does this force you to say that all modern things are forbidden and that we would be impractically paralyzed in our daily lives into non-action?

38. Make a one- or two-page outline of the content of Chapter 17 for sermon or other presentation use. Then, using this, explain how passages in Hebrews teach that Bible silence forbids. Start with an explanation of the figure on page 115, consulting Chapter 11. Then relate each Hebrews passage studied in Chapter 17 to this figure.

39. Explain and reply to the Bible silence permits claims in Chapter 18.
40. Explain and reply to the Bible silence permits claims in Chapter 19.
41. Explain and reply to the Bible silence permits claims in Chapter 20.

PART 3: RELATED TOPICS

42. Who violates the don't add to or take away from passages, the defender of Bible silence forbids or the defender of Bible silence permits? Explain.
43. Explain the Bible silence forbids claim which is based on 2 Cor 5:7a with Rom 10:17.
44. Explain the Bible silence forbids claim which is based on Jn 4:24 with Jn 17:17.
45. Explain the Bible silence forbids claim which is based on Mk 7:7-9. Does Col 2:22-23 teach Bible silence forbids along the same lines as Mk 7:7-9? Does Jer 10:23?
46. Do you know of other Bible silence forbids claims? If so, identify them and explain.
47. Do you know of other Bible silence permits claims? If so, identify them and explain.
48. Identify the three laws expressed by what Chapter 22 calls the "T".
49. Chapter 22 refers to the "horizontal" law of exclusion. What are other ways this is expressed? (See Chapter 19.)
50. Explain and illustrate the "horizontal" law of exclusion as J. D. Thomas expresses it in *We Be Brethren*.
51. Explain the refutation of this "law" as expressed in Chapter 22.
52. Explain the ambiguity in the expression "To specify is to exclude" as mentioned in Chapter 22.

53. Explain your reply to the following: Either requiring a specific action has the power to exclude (forbid) all other specifics under the same generic, or it does not. So does it or doesn't it? If you answer "It does," then you are saying statements like "You must buy apples" implies "You must not buy pears, or bananas, or any other kind of fruit." (Remember the meaning of implies.) So, this "law" of exclusion, if true, would result in many conflicting Bible passages.

54. Chapter 22 compares two clusters of principles. Explain how they differ.

55. Someone says, "Please give a precisely stated argument which shows that a required generic implies authority for all specifics under it (except of course for any of these specifics which the Bible elsewhere forbids.) For example, show authority for church buildings."

First, consider the following argument. (Understand that 'all specifics are permitted" is to be appended with "except any specific which the Bible addresses as a forbidden action.)

A. Either *all specifics under a required generic are required* or *forbidden* or *permitted*.
   This statement is true because it exhausts all possibilities. So one of the mentioned possibilities must be the truth.

B. It is false that *all specifics are required*.
   Requiring all the specifics is impossible to follow. For example, using every possible specific of fruit of the vine is not possible. This would include all possible temperatures, all possible quantities, all possible shades of color, etc. It cannot be that an all-knowing fair God requires the impossible. So statement B is true.

C. It is false that *all specifics are forbidden.*
If all the specifics were forbidden, then the required generic would be impossible to do. So statement C is true.

D. Therefore, *all specifics under a required generic are permitted.*

Since the other two possibilities are false, then the only one left (namely, all specifics are permitted) must be the truth. So, for example, all variations of taking fruit of the vine are authorized by the generic requirement in 1 Cor 11:24-25 (except any specific implementation which would violate 1 Cor 6:9-10).

Second, consider the following: Since (A1) Heb 10:25 requires Christians to assemble some place and (B1) the passage is not specific as to where, then (C1) the passage provides us with a required generic for assembling.

If both statements and C1 and D (above) are true, does it follow that Heb 10:25 authorizes church buildings? Are both statements C1 and D true?

Using reasoning like the above, discuss the following:

- Does Eph 5:18-19 authorize song books?
- Does Mk 16:15-16 authorize radio?
- Does 1 Tim 5:8 authorize computers?
- Does 1 Tim 4:8 authorize the use of modern exercise equipment? (Note that this passage teaches that bodily exercise has **some** profit and not **no** profit. Are there Biblical exceptions to exercising?)

56. In a Bible concordance, look up the word "rest." Define briefly the words found and note the passages. Discuss whether any of these passages authorizes various recreational activities today.

57. Gen 1:28 talks about subduing the earth. One commentator says of this verse: "The commission thus received was to utilize for his necessities the vast resources of the earth, by agricultural and mining operations, by geographical research, scientific discovery, and mechanical invention."[211] Discuss:
   - What specific kinds of human activities this includes. (That is, identify several specifics under this generic.),
   - Does Ps 8:6 teach the same principle?, and
   - Whether or not this principle expressed in the OT scriptures also has application in our (NT) age. Is Heb 2:5-8 relevant?

58. Do the Bible passages which teach how to be saved (for example, passages like Rev 22:17, Rom 10:17, Acts 17:30-31, Rom 10:9-10 and Acts 22:16) **imply** that the doctrine about immersing infants unto forgiveness is false doctrine? Then is the Bible silent on such infant baptism?

59. Is the practice of sprinkling as a substitution for immersing unto the remission of sins an example of where the Bible is silent?

60. Consider this:
   Some Bible passages are generic but would be misused if applied to all human activities. This is the case because God has built fences around some areas of human activity, thus setting them off from others. For example, 1 Cor 13 gives us the generic

---

[211] Thomas Whitelaw, *Genesis*, ed., H.D. M Spence and Joseph S. Exell, The Pulpit Commentary (rpt. Grand Rapids: Wm B. Eerdmans Publishing Company, 1950), p. 31.

that we are to love. But this does not authorize us to worship God any way we want, so long as it is motivated by our love for Him. As to worship, we must add Jn 4:24 to the love requirement. The passage teaches that we **must** worship God in spirit in and truth. So God has built a fence around worship. Sexual activity is another area around which God built a fence. He calls that fence "marriage." 1 Cor 7 and Mt 19 are two passages, among others, which show this.

Another way of saying this is that some generic requirements are AND'ed with other requirements. This narrows the acceptable field of activity, because now we have more than one requirement regarding the actions in question. To require that we meet obligation A with obligation B is more restrictive than to require that we meet only obligation A.

Now explain why the following are true or false:

- Acts 10:15 is a required generic authorizing the eating of all kinds of meat, without the dietary restrictions like in the OT. But this required generic does not authorize eating meat during the partaking of the Lord's supper.

- Rom 13:8-9 is a generic requirement that we love people. And Mt 7:12 is sometimes called the golden rule. It is a required generic for doing unto another what you would have the other do to you. But either passage would be misapplied if one were to claim "It authorizes specific sexual activities between consenting adults who are not married to each other."

-◆ ◆ ◆-